A LIFEGUIDE BIBLE STUDY

1 CORINTHIANS

The Challenges of Life Together

13 Studies
for individuals or groups

Paul Stevens & Dan Williams

With Notes for Leaders

INTERVARSITY PRESS
DOWNERS GROVE, ILLINOIS 60515

InterVarsity Press is the book-publishing division of InterVarsity Christian Fellowship, a student movement active on campus at hundreds of universities, colleges and schools of nursing. For information about local and regional activities, write Public Relations Dept., InterVarsity Christian Fellowship, 6400 Schroeder Rd., P.O. Box 7895, Madison, WI 53707-7895.

All Scripture quotations, unless otherwise indicated, are taken from the Holy Bible, New International Version. Copyright © 1973, 1978, International Bible Society. Used by permission of Zondervan Bible Publishers.

Cover photograph: Connie Toops

ISBN 0-8308-1009-9

Printed in the United States of America

18	17	16	15	14	13	12	11	10	9	8	7	6	5
99	98	97	96	95	94	93	92						

Contents

Getting the Most from LifeGuide Bible Studies

Many of us long to fill our minds and our lives with Scripture. We desire to be transformed by its message. LifeGuide Bible Studies are designed to be an exciting and challenging way to do just that. They help us to be guided by God's Word in every area of life.

How They Work
LifeGuides have a number of distinctive features. Perhaps the most important is that they are *inductive* rather than *deductive*. In other words, they lead us to *discover* what the Bible says rather than simply *telling* us what it says.

They are also thought provoking. They help us to think about the meaning of the passage so that we can truly understand what the author is saying. The questions require more than one-word answers.

The studies are personal. Questions expose us to the promises, assurances, exhortations and challenges of God's Word. They are designed to allow the Scriptures to renew our minds so that we can be transformed by the Spirit of God. This is the ultimate goal of all Bible study.

The studies are versatile. They are designed for student, neighborhood and church groups. They are also effective for individual study.

How They're Put Together
LifeGuides also have a distinctive format. Each study need take no more than forty-five minutes in a group setting or thirty minutes in personal study—unless you choose to take more time.

The studies can be used within a quarter system in a church and fit well in a semester or trimester system on a college campus. If a guide has more than thirteen studies, it is divided into two or occasionally three parts of approximately twelve studies each.

LifeGuides use a workbook format. Space is provided for writing answers to each question. This is ideal for personal study and allows group members to prepare in advance for the discussion.

The studies also contain leader's notes. They show how to lead a group discussion, provide additional background information on certain questions, give helpful tips on group dynamics and suggest ways to deal with problems which may arise during the discussion. With such helps, someone with little or no experience can lead an effective study.

Suggestions for Individual Study

1. As you begin each study, pray that God will help you to understand and apply the passage to your life.

2. Read and reread the assigned Bible passage to familiarize yourself with what the author is saying. In the case of book studies, you may want to read through the entire book prior to the first study. This will give you a helpful overview of its contents.

3. A good modern translation of the Bible, rather than the King James Version or a paraphrase, will give you the most help. The New International Version, the New American Standard Bible and the Revised Standard Version are all recommended. However, the questions in this guide are based on the New International Version.

4. Write your answers in the space provided in the study guide. This will help you to express your understanding of the passage clearly.

5. It might be good to have a Bible dictionary handy. Use it to look up any unfamiliar words, names or places.

Suggestions for Group Study

1. Come to the study prepared. Follow the suggestions for individual study mentioned above. You will find that careful preparation will greatly enrich your time spent in group discussion.

2. Be willing to participate in the discussion. The leader of your group will not be lecturing. Instead, he or she will be encouraging the members of the group to discuss what they have learned from the passage. The leader will be asking the questions that are found in this guide. Plan to share what God has taught you in your individual study.

3. Stick to the passage being studied. Your answers should be based on the verses which are the focus of the discussion and not on outside authorities such as commentaries or speakers. This guide deliberately avoids jumping

from book to book or passage to passage. Each study focuses on only one passage. Book studies are generally designed to lead you through the book in the order in which it was written. This will help you follow the author's argument.

4. Be sensitive to the other members of the group. Listen attentively when they share what they have learned. You may be surprised by their insights! Link what you say to the comments of others so the group stays on the topic. Also, be affirming whenever you can. This will encourage some of the more hesitant members of the group to participate.

5. Be careful not to dominate the discussion. We are sometimes so eager to share what we have learned that we leave too little opportunity for others to respond. By all means participate! But allow others to also.

6. Expect God to teach you through the passage being discussed and through the other members of the group. Pray that you will have an enjoyable and profitable time together.

7. If you are the discussion leader, you will find additional suggestions and helpful ideas for each study in the leader's notes. These are found at the back of the guide.

Introducing 1 Corinthians

In 1938, just before World War 2, Dietrich Bonhoeffer wrote *Life Together*, a moving little book on the principles of Christian community. Eighteen and a half centuries earlier the apostle Paul wrote what has come to be known as 1 Corinthians, a fascinating commentary on one Christian community which he founded. Why should we bother with either of these books?

Simply because we all have to live together with people, in Christian contexts and otherwise. Whether the situation involves a close friendship, a roommate, a spouse, a small group, a family, an office, a campus club, a neighborhood or a congregation, the challenges of life together will inevitably crop up. Church life is not immune to these problems, and Corinth was particularly susceptible. As a result, we can benefit from Paul's advice to that community.

Are there cliques and power struggles in the communities of which you are a part? Are you plagued by people who think they are spiritually or intellectually superior? How do you handle the immorality that seems so prevalent in the world, especially when it begins to invade the church? What is the proper way to exercise your rights, especially when a friend wrongs you or you feel that a matter of principle is at stake? How do we regulate marriage and singleness in the face of so many attacks on the health of both these life-situations? How are we ever going to solve the battle of the sexes? What is the path to respecting one another's personality and gifts? Can eternity make a difference in how we live together today?

If any of these questions are relevant to your life and communities, then 1 Corinthians has something to say to you.

The relationship between Paul and the church at Corinth is a bittersweet chapter in church history. As the apostle traveled down the isthmus joining the two halves of Achaia (Greece) and first spotted the plain surrounding the city and the hill known as the Acrocorinth jutting up behind, he could hardly have imagined the depths and heights that would be reached by the church he left behind eighteen months later (see Acts 18 for the background of this part of Paul's second missionary journey). Nor could Paul have any idea of the depths and heights of emotion to which the members of that church would lead him, their spiritual father, over the next few years of visits and letters.

Both comedy and tragedy are found in the story of the Corinthian church. There was the comedy of a dynamic, gifted Christian community composed of uneducated, uninfluential people. They were plucked out of one of the greatest centers of trade, political authority and pagan religion in the Roman empire. Morals were so bad in that city that its citizens had inspired a word for sexual license—to *Corinthianize!* The existence of a church in such a setting was a reason for comic rejoicing.

However, there was also the tragedy of the Corinthians forgetting their humble roots and placing themselves as kings over one another—even over Paul their founder and friend. The resulting tensions and schisms would boil over with even greater heartache for Paul in 2 Corinthians.

In the first six chapters of 1 Corinthians Paul begins with the distressing matters he has learned about: factions, incest, court cases, and freedom gone wild. In chapters 7—14 he treats a series of topics that the Corinthians have asked him about, from marriage to spiritual gifts, with each new topic signaled by the phrase *Now concerning. . . .* Finally, he sums up the teaching of the book in chapter 15, which is devoted to a theology of the resurrection or "last things."

Understanding why chapter 15 and parts of chapters 1—4 fit in this book is the key to unlocking 1 Corinthians. As always, Paul is not only interested in correcting practice, but also in grounding his instruction in theological principles. In fact, the Corinthians had two root problems: premature spirituality (they thought they had everything heaven could offer) and immature spirituality (they forgot that the heart of the gospel is love, servanthood and the cross). Perhaps our communities, too, need correction in both practice and theology.

For the sake of simplicity and brevity, this study guide generally treats 1 Corinthians chapter by chapter. On three occasions we combined two chapters of the book into one study. We will rely on some cross-references and the Leader's Notes to clarify thematic overlaps from chapter to chapter, while concentrating on the subjects as they arise naturally in the letter.

If the topics seem to appear haphazardly, try to keep in mind the underlying theological issues at stake throughout the letter. And remember that most of our relationships and communities are pretty haphazard affairs themselves!

3-20-97 Prayer Requests
* Growth in the Study
* Bible + Life
* Steve
* Wednesday Study

April
11,12,13
$25

1

Called in Christ:

Saints Made of Clay Not Plaster

1 Corinthians 1:1-31

Have you ever found a Christian group that doesn't have any problems? If so, don't join it—you'll ruin everything!

The church in Corinth was far from perfect. Paul had heard a long list of complaints about this eager but misguided flock. As he attempted some long-distance pastoring, where would he begin? Paul's starting-point is very relevant for problem groups and individuals today.

1. "A corpse has no problems." How does this maxim help you understand the everyday life of your church or fellowship?

something that is not living or moving or breathing

2. Read 1 Corinthians 1:1-9. Before discussing the problems in Corinth, Paul affirms his readers. Why is he thankful for them?

spiritual gifts
- they're being enriched by God in speaking + knowledge.
- their testimony about Christ was confirmed

3. Read 1:10-17. Why do you think cliques had formed around Paul, Apollos and Cephas (v. 12)?

they were religious leaders that the people looked up to "denominations"

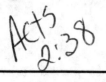

What do you think the "Christ" party represents (assuming it is not something positive)?

They were the people who "knew" christ better than any one else

4. Why would such cliques stir up quarrels (v. 11)?

because everyon's "leader" is the one to follow. no one elses is rght

5. How did Paul conduct himself in Corinth to avoid, if possible, the problem of a personality cult (vv. 14-17)?

he didnt baptize people

6. What evidence of hero worship do you observe in the church today?

* musicians
* youth pastors
* athletes

Why is hero worship foolish (v. 13)?

Because no one but christ was crucified for our sins

7. Read 1:18-31. The Corinthians boasted in worldly wisdom and those who taught it. How does the message of the cross destroy all such boasting (vv. 18-25)?

VS. 31
Let him who boasts boast in the Lord.

8. The Corinthians also felt intellectually and spiritually superior to others. What had they forgotten about their past and the reason God chose them (vv. 26-29)? *were born a normal birth*
- weak
- lowliness

9. As you reflect on your own past, what reasons do you have for being humble rather than proud?

10. How can genuine humility promote unity in your church or fellowship?

11. What does it mean to "boast in the Lord" (vv. 30-31)?

12. Take time to thank the Lord for all he has done for you.

2
Mind of Christ:
True Wisdom from the Spirit

1 Corinthians 2:1—3:4

Many people think Christianity is for the mindless and dull. Someone has said, "I feel like unscrewing my head and putting it underneath the pew everytime I go to church." Unfortunately, this chapter has been used to support an uneducated, unthinking approach to Christianity. But this misses Paul's point. As Sören Kierkegaard, the Danish philosopher, once said: Christ doesn't destroy reason; he *dethrones* it.

1. How has Christianity challenged you intellectually?

2. Read 1 Corinthians 2:1-5. Greek philosophers were often polished orators whose eloquence and wisdom dazzled their audiences. How does this contrast with Paul's preaching in Corinth?

* Paul came in weakness and fear
  with much trembelling
* but with a demonstration of the spirit's
  power

3. Why didn't Paul rely on his great wisdom and his obvious communication skills?

because he didnt want
to be like everyone else

4. How have Christians today adopted the world's methods in spreading the gospel?
- selling christ
- through media - TV, music, news paper
- bumper stickers

When do these tools become worldly

5. Read 2:6-16. How is God's wisdom different from the wisdom of this age (vv. 6-10)?
- secret
- has been hidden

Why are *secret* and *hidden* good words to describe this wisdom?

6. If God's wisdom is secret and hidden, how can we come to know it (vv. 10-13)?
because when we receive the Holy Spirit

7. When it comes to understanding God's wisdom, how does the person without the Spirit contrast with the spiritual person (vv. 14-16)?
w/o - spiritual things seem foolish to him

8. If non-Christians cannot understand the things of the Spirit, how can we talk with them about Christ?

9. Read 3:1-4. Even though the Corinthians had the Spirit, why couldn't they be considered spiritual?

because they were still too young.

10. Based on this passage (2:1—3:4), how would you define spiritual maturity?

11. Which category best describes you: a person without the Spirit (2:14), an infant in Christ (3:1), a worldly Christian (3:1) or a spiritual Christian (2:15; 3:1)? Explain.

12. What can you do to become more spiritually mature?

3
Founded on Christ:
Indwelt by the Spirit

1 Corinthians 3:5-23

The Duke of Windsor, recalling his childhood discipline by George V, then King of England, said that his father used to daily remind him, "Never forget who you are." As the spiritual father of the Corinthians, Paul reminds them in this chapter, "Never forget *whose* you are."

The Corinthians were worldly and quarrelsome because they misunderstood both the message and the messengers of the cross. In chapters one and two, Paul focused on the message—the true wisdom from God. Now he looks at God's messengers. As he does so, Paul reminds the Corinthians and us of our true identity in Christ.

1. Think of a time when someone who really cared for you confronted you with a failure to live up to your highest. What qualities of that encounter made it constructive?

2. Read 1 Corinthians 3:4-23. What two illustrations does Paul use to describe himself and Apollos (vv. 6-9, 10-15)?

What does Paul compare the church to in each of these illustrations (see also vv. 16-17)?

3. In what ways is God's church like a field being planted (vv. 6-9)?

Why is it foolish to exalt those who work in the field?

4. In 3:10-15 Paul changes the metaphor from farming to building. Describe the various ways the church is like a building under construction.

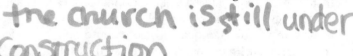
the church is still under Construction

5. What does it mean to be careful how one builds (v. 10)?

6. How will the quality of our work be revealed on the day of judgment?

7. How does this way of evaluating our lives apply not only to so-called Christian work but also to other aspects of our vocation in Christ: relationships, occupations, avocations, community involvement and so on?

8. In verse 3 Paul accused the Corinthians of being worldly. How can he say to the same people, "You are God's temple" and "God's Spirit lives in you" (v. 16)?

Because of God's Grace

9. What kind of destruction of the temple is Paul thinking about in verse 17?

How do you see Christian communities being destroyed this way today?

★ Christ centered
★ Media

10. The Corinthians had initially claimed "I belong to Paul" or "I belong to Apollos" (1:12 RSV). Paul claims something more important. In what sense do Paul, Apollos and everything else belong to the Corinthians—and to us (3:21-23)?

Because God is our Dad

Why should this put an end to "boasting about men" (v. 21)?

★ doesn't give God credit
★ isn't edifying to the body

11. How does this chapter affect your view of your own ministry in the church and that of professional ministers?

4
Servants of Christ:
At the End of the Procession
1 Corinthians 4:1-21

In the last study Paul called the Corinthians not to forget that they were God's holy temple. Now he calls them and all Christian communities to experience the power of radical servanthood for Christ's sake. St. Francis of Assisi exhibited this when he walked through Moslem battle lines during the Crusades in order to preach to the Sultan. Mother Teresa also is a "fool for Christ" when she bends down to care for a dying beggar in Calcutta. There is power in such actions, even though the wise ones of this age shake their heads in disbelief or wag their tongues in scorn.

1. How do you feel when you hear about people like St. Francis who give away all they have to the poor, or who live sacrificially, like Mother Teresa?

2. Read 1 Corinthians 4:1-7. In contrast to the hero worship in Corinth, how do Paul and his coworkers wish to be regarded (vv. 1-2)?

Above all else, why do you think God requires faithfulness from his servants (v. 2)?

3. What standards do we often use to judge God's servants today?

- How *much they do.*
- How big their following"
- How popular - used by denominations

Why does Paul care very little about such judgments (vv. 3-5)?

Because "It is the Lord who judges me"

4. Paul fears the Corinthians are moving "beyond what was written"— probably a reference to the Old Testament Scriptures. How might going beyond the authority of Scripture result in taking "pride in one man over against another" (v. 6)?

What does the proud person fail to realize (v. 7)?

they arent different from any one else

5. Read verses 8-17. Scripture teaches that the suffering of this present age precedes the glory of the age to come. In their own minds, how had the Corinthians taken a short cut to glory (vv. 8, 10)?

How did their "glorious" description of themselves contrast with the experiences of Paul and the other apostles (vv. 9-13)?

6. Why would the Corinthians and the world look down on the apostles rather than viewing them as great?

7. If you were one of the Corinthians, how would Paul's words make you feel ashamed or warned (v. 14) about your attitudes?

8. How would imitating Paul's way of life (vv. 16-17) require changes in your thinking and actions?

9. Read verses 18-21. We receive the first hint in this section that some in Corinth were not only boasting about other leaders but were also putting down Paul. How does the apostle choose to combat these opponents?

10. Paul is no stranger to miraculous acts and miraculous speech. But in light of chapters 1—4, what kind of kingdom power do you think Paul hopes to find when he arrives in Corinth (vv. 18-21)?

Which is the best symbol for such power—a whip or a loving, gentle spirit? Why?

11. In what ways does this passage challenge you to become a "fool for Christ"?

5
Members of Christ:
The Body Is Meant for the Lord
1 Corinthians 5:1—6:20

T he New Testament church has inspired both exciting and disasterous experiments down through history. Hoping to create the perfect New Testament community, some have tried to design groups where all the gifts are expressed, worship is spontaneous and fellowship is deep. But they forget the common element of all New Testament churches—problems!

In chapters 1—4 Paul dealt with divisions in the church. Now he focuses on serious moral problems in Corinth. Incest and drunkenness during communion are hardly what we hope to find in church. But we must remember that growing churches are not always filled with well-scrubbed Christians, but rather with a motley collection of sinners being saved.

1. How do you react when you hear about serious moral and spiritual problems of people in your church?

2. Read 1 Corinthians 5:1-8. In Greece there was no shame in having sexual relationships before marriage or outside of marriage. Demosthenes writes: "We keep mistresses for pleasure, concubines for the day-to-day needs of the body, but we have wives in order to produce children legitimately and to have a trustworthy guardian of our homes." What made the sexual problem in this church especially loathsome to Paul?

3. How is Paul's strategy of discipline designed to bring health to both the church and the individual (vv. 2-5)?

Why do you think so few churches today practice this kind of discipline?

4. Paul compares the Christian life to the Passover and Feast of Unleavened Bread (see Ex 12). According to Paul, what do the yeast, the bread without yeast and the Passover lamb symbolize (vv. 6-8)?

How does this analogy help us relate to people who bring their pre-Christian lifestyles into the church?

5. Read 5:9-13. Some Christians practice a doctrine of "double separation." First, they separate themselves from the evil influences in the world. Second, they separate themselves from Christians who have not separated themselves from the world. What type of separation is taught in these verses?

Why is associating with immoral people in the church more dangerous than keeping company with immoral people in secular society?

6. Read 6:1-11. What commands and guidelines does Paul give for settling disputes between Christians (vv. 1-8)? Explain.

7. In verses 9-10 Paul mentions the kinds of people who will not inherit the kingdom of God. Why do you think he warns us against being deceived about this (v. 9)?

8. How and why had the Corinthians changed since becoming Christians (v. 11)?

9. How can we distinguish between the kinds of people who should be put out of the church (5:2, 9-11; 6:9-10) and those who belong in the church even though they are "worldly" and immature (see 3:1)?

10. Read 6:12-20. "Everything is permissible for me" (v. 12) was probably a quote from some Corinthians who felt they were above moral rules and that their bodies had nothing to do with their spiritual lives. What arguments does Paul use to refute this idea?

11. Paul calls the body "a temple of the Holy Spirit" (vv. 18-20). How does the biblical view of the body presented here contrast with our modern view?

How can understanding your body as a temple of the Holy Spirit (v. 19) lead to a healthy balance of bodily control and bodily celebration?

12. Ask God to help you take whatever steps are necessary to maintain both personal and corporate purity.

6
Devoted to Christ:
Marrying When Time is Short
1 Corinthians 7:1-40

Corinth, unlike most modern cities today, did not have sex shops, *Playboy* magazines, porn videos and "adult entertainment" centers. But there was so much sexual immorality that the ancients had a word to describe engaging in raw sensual pleasure—to *Corinthianize*. In chapter six Paul dealt with those who justified a permissive lifestyle in the name of Christian freedom. In this chapter he battles on the opposite front. Some Corinthians claimed sex was sinful—or at least a second-class diversion—even in marriage. In response Paul answers questions about marriage, sexuality and singleness.

1. What types of questions do Christians today ask about sex and marriage?

2. Read 1 Corinthians 7:1-9, where Paul answers questions about sex. Although Paul agrees that celibacy is good (v. 1), why is it impractical for most people (vv. 2, 7)?

3. What practical advice does Paul give to the unmarried and the married for avoiding sexual immorality (vv. 2-9)?

4. Paul's emphasis is not on what a spouse should expect but what a spouse should give (vv. 3-5). Why is this emphasis important?

5. Read 7:10-16, where Paul answers questions about marriage and divorce. How do his statements "to the married" (vv. 10-11) affirm what the Lord had already taught (see Mk 10:2-12)?

6. In verses 12-16 Paul discusses a situation not covered by the Lord—marriages between Christians and non-Christians. Why might a Christian be tempted to divorce a non-Christian?

According to Paul, what are some benefits of remaining in a mixed marriage? Explain.

7. Under what circumstances would Paul seemingly allow for divorce, and why (vv. 15-16)?

Why is Paul's instruction here not an "easy way out"?

---

8. What principles from this passage could help us care for Christians who are considering separation or divorce?

---

9. Read 7:17-24, where Paul counsels those who think they are in the wrong situation. How does Paul explain and illustrate the "rule" that applies to such people?

---

10. Paul speaks of God calling us *to* a certain situation (vv. 17, 24) and of God calling us while we were *in* that situation (vv. 18-22). How are these two dimensions of calling different?

What difference should being called by God make if we are in a difficult marriage or an unsatisfying job?

---

11. Read verses 24-40, where Paul addresses *those considering marriage.* Why does Paul call singleness a "better" way (v. 38) and a "happier" way (v. 40) when he has such a high view of marriage?

12. Taking the chapter as a whole, what considerations would help a couple decide whether to marry, to wait or to separate?

13. Ask God to help you to be faithful to him in your relationships, your job and the other areas of your life.

7
Living for Christ:
The Right to Relinquish Rights
1 Corinthians 8:1—9:27

A note tacked up on a refrigerator had these words: "It is better to be righteous than right!" Today individuals and groups are clamoring and clashing over rights: the right to free speech, the rights of the poor, the right to liberation, women's rights, aboriginal rights, the right to not be bothered by smokers (or nonsmokers), the rights of animals, the rights of Blacks, the rights of Whites.

So many of the struggles over rights, both legitimate and bogus, seem to revolve around attaining freedom to change the status quo. The apostle Paul, however, appears to be on opposite ground. He has just written about remaining in the situation God calls us to, whether that be slavery or singleness, and concentrating on keeping God's commands (7:17-24). Now we will see that Paul indeed practices what he preaches. For him rights and freedoms are unimportant compared to the privilege of living for Christ.

1. How do you react when you know you are right, and yet someone continues openly to oppose you?

2. Read 1 Corinthians 8:1-13. Sacrificial animals offered in temples were dedicated to a pagan god, and most of them were sold in the public market.

Understandably, many Christians in Corinth wondered whether they should eat such meat. According to Paul, what do mature Christians know about food sacrificed to idols (vv. 4-6, 8)?

What warning does Paul give about this kind of knowledge (vv. 1-3)? Explain.

3. What does Paul say is more important than exercising the freedom that comes from knowledge (vv. 9-13)?

4. In what situations today might our "knowledge" and freedom destroy a weaker brother?

What distinguishes actions which challenge the immature to grow from actions which wound them?

5. Read 9:1-27. Paul moves on from rights and freedoms based on *knowledge* to the topic of rights based on *position*. What apostolic rights has Paul given up (vv. 4-5, 11-12, 14, 18-19)?

6. How can receiving financial benefits, even a mere living, from being a preacher sometimes hinder the gospel (v. 12)?

7. What things in your life might be hindering the spread of the gospel?

8. How does giving up his right to financial support allow Paul to "boast" and to expect a reward he would not receive otherwise (vv. 15-18)?

9. In what ways might we go beyond the call of duty as Christians in order to receive a heavenly reward?

10. How and why has Paul given up the freedom to live whatever lifestyle he prefers (vv. 19-23)?

11. How might we adjust our lifestyles in order to reach people in various subcultures?

12. In giving up the rights mentioned in chapters 8—9, how are we like athletes in training (vv. 24-27)?

Ask God to help you train more rigorously so you will not be disqualified but will receive the victor's crown.

8
Eating with Christ:
All for the Glory of God
1 Corinthians 10:1-33

Should Christians go to R-rated movies—or any movies for that matter? Should they drink alcoholic beverages such as beer or wine? Should they wear expensive clothes, makeup and jewelry? Debates over such "questionable" practices are as old as the church. How can we resolve them?

The Corinthians were divided over such issues. Some had overscrupulous consciences. They would not sit down to a meal if the meat had been purchased at a pagan meat market (and therefore offered to a "god"). Others were so "liberated" that they could eat the Lord's Supper and then commit sexual immorality. These liberated Christians regarded baptism and the eucharist (communion) as automatic protection against God's judgment. In 1 Corinthians 10 Paul finds a way of reaching both kinds of people: he calls them and us to do everything for the glory of God.

1. What "questionable" practices have you wrestled with personally?

2. Read 1 Corinthians 10:1-13. What experiences did all the Israelites have in common when they left Egypt and headed for the Promised Land?

Why was God not pleased with them?

---

3. Why does Paul remind the Corinthians (and us) of these events?

---

4. How does Paul counter the idea that some temptations are just too strong to be resisted?

---

5. Think of one or two areas where you are currently experiencing temptation. In which one of these are you least likely to believe that there is a way of escape?

In what way has God provided an escape for your temptation?

---

6. Read 10:14-22. Why are some lifestyles incompatable with celebrating the Lord's Supper?

---

7. Although Paul is dealing with a pastoral problem rather than doctrine, what does he teach us about the sacredness of the Lord's Supper?

8. Read 10:23-33. According to these verses, what principles should guide our behavior as Christians?

How does Paul apply these principles to the subject of eating meat offered to idols?

9. What practices in your life do you consider "permissible" but possibly not beneficial or constructive (v. 23)?

10. How can the principles discussed in this passage guide your behavior in these specific areas?

The Christian is a most free lord of all, subject to none. The Christian is a most submissive servant, subject to all. (Martin Luther)

9
Headship of Christ:
We Are Interdependent
1 Corinthians 11:1-34

Two trends in Western society contrive to make us independent people:
the trend to blur the differences between the sexes (androgyny) and the
human potential movement. In the movie *Tootsie* a male actor impersonating
a woman said to a woman with whom he fell in love, "I was a better man
with you when I was a woman than I am a woman with you now that I am
a man." Such is the sexual confusion produced by the first trend. Fritz Perls
verbalized the second trend this way: "I do my thing and you do your thing
and if by chance we meet, it's beautiful."

Both trends work against our newness in Christ. Followers of Jesus are
neither independent nor dependent but *inter*dependent. In 1 Corinthians 10
(study 8) we explored our interdependence in matters of conscience. Now
we discover interdependence in Christian worship.

1. When you enter a worship service, do you tend to think mainly of your
personal relationship to God or your relationship with your fellow worshipers? Explain.

2. Read 1 Corinthians 11:1-15. What seems to be Paul's major concern for the
church in this section?

3. The word *head* in verse 3 could mean either "chief" and "ruler" or "source" and "origin" (like the head of a stream). Which understanding of headship best fits Paul's concern here? Explain.

4. In light of the headship described in verse 3, why was it wrong for a man to pray or prophesy with his head covered (vv. 4-10)?

5. In the culture of Corinth a woman signaled that she was in right relationship with her husband either by wearing a veil which covered her hair or by wearing her hair up (rather than letting it fall loose). What reasons does Paul give for continuing this practice (vv. 4-10, 13-16)?

6. Head coverings also symbolized the differences between the sexes. According to Paul, what differences between men and women have been built into creation by God himself (vv. 7-10)?

7. Paul balances his previous statements by saying that "in the Lord" man is not independent of woman (vv. 11-12). Why is this balance important?

8. Although we may not have a cultural equivalent for head coverings, how should appropriate relationships between men and women be expressed in Christian community?

9. Read 11:17-34. In New Testament times communion was celebrated during a common meal or "love feast." What abuses had crept into this celebration (vv. 18-22)?

10. What is the purpose and significance of the Lord's Supper (vv. 23-26)?

In the light of this, why would eating and drinking "without recognizing the body of the Lord" be so dangerous (vv. 29-32)?

12. According to Paul, how can we eat and drink the Lord's Supper in a worthy manner (v. 28-33)?

13. What has this chapter taught you about worship that is honoring or dishonoring to God?

10
Body of Christ:
Manifestations of the Spirit
1 Corinthians 12:1-31

Imagine designing a church in which most members sit passively, where one or two gifts are exalted and others are made to feel dispensable. Sound familiar?

The church today has enormous frozen assets. Only when we thaw these assets and release every member for ministry can the work of God be done in the world. After several decades of "gift" teaching, we have made surprisingly little progress. One reason is that gifts have been co-opted by the human potential movement. We view our gifts as part of our development and fulfillment rather than as one more glorious way to be interdependent in Christ. This passage focuses on the true nature and purpose of spiritual gifts.

1. How do you respond when you are told that you have a gift or talent which the group vitally needs?

2. Read 1 Corinthians 12:1-11. What particular problem in the Corinthian church may have led Paul to offer the "test" in verse 3?

What clue does Paul's test give us about the ultimate goal of spiritual gifts?

_____

3. What do verses 4-6 reveal about the unity and diversity of spiritual gifts?

_____

4. Paul calls each gift a "manifestation of the Spirit" (v. 7). In what ways does the Spirit manifest himself in the church, and why (vv. 7-11)?

_____

5. Read 12:12-26. What might make some members of your church feel useless or envious of other parts of the body?

How does Paul respond to such people (vv. 14-20)?

_____

7. What might make some members of your church feel self-sufficient or superior (v. 21)?

_____

8. According to Paul, how can we make every part of the body feel special (vv. 21-26)?

How could you apply these principles in your church or group?

9. Read 12:27-31. Paul does not give us a complete list of gifts in this chapter. What might the words *first, second, third* and *then* (v. 28) indicate?

10. How do you reconcile Paul's exhortation to "eagerly desire the greater gifts" (v. 31) with his earlier emphasis that God sovereignly assigns gifts (vv. 11, 18, 28)?

Do you think this is a *personal* exhortation, something for the whole Christian community to hear, or both?

11. What can you do to help others in your group or church to discover their giftedness?

What do you think will happen to your own gift when you do this?

Sir, you wish to serve God and go to heaven. Then you must find companions or make them, for the Bible knows nothing of solitary religion. (Advice given to John Wesley)

11
Love of Christ:
The Most Excellent Way

1 Corinthians 13:1-13

The psychiatrist R. D. Laing says that "we are effectively destroying ourselves by violence masquerading as love."* Perhaps the most abused phrase in the English language is "I love you." Instead of communicating unselfish caring, it often expresses enlightened self-interest, manipulative affection or sheer lust.

In 1 Corinthians 13 Paul not only defines love for us but shows us why this is the most excellent way to relate to anyone—especially to members of the family of God. Following his treatment of spiritual gifts in 1 Corinthians 12, Paul seems to say, "If you are confused about gifts, just love!" This is one absolute that is not obsolete.

1. Think of a person who has truly loved you. What were the marks of that person's way of relating to you?

2. Read 1 Corinthians 13. This chapter has been called "a pure and perfect gem, perhaps the noblest assemblage of beautiful thoughts in beautiful language extant in our world" (H. Alford). What are your main impressions after reading the chapter as a whole?

3. What is so tragic about using our gifts without love (vv. 1-3)?

How can we know whether our personal ministry is so loveless?

4. How would you define each of love's qualities (vv. 4-7)?

5. Which aspect of love do you most need to develop?

6. Besides telling us what love is, this passage gives us an incidental portrait of Jesus as the ultimate lover. Reread verses 4-7, replacing *love* with *Jesus*. What fresh picture of Jesus' care do you gain through this exercise?

7. In verses 8-13 Paul summarizes the *supremacy of love*. Compared with love, why do the gifts have limited value?

8. Some understand the "perfection" in verse 10 as the completed New Testament, thus eliminating the need for tongues or prophecy today. Others understand it as the perfection we will experience when Christ returns. In light of Paul's other comparisons (vv. 11-12), which interpretation seems more likely? Explain.

9. Why is love greater than faith or hope (v. 13)?

10. Why is love the ultimate solution to the divisions in Corinth or in any church?

11. How can love lead to healthy interdependence in our relationships rather than unhealthy independence or dependence?

Love is not a gift. . . . It lies at the very heart of all gifts. (A. Bittlinger. *Gifts and Graces* [Grand Rapids: Eerdmans. 1967], p. 75)

12
Speaking for Christ:
Adult Thinking and Orderly Worship
1 Corinthians 14:1-40

Words are cheap today. They can be digitized and processed. With one depressed button on a computer we can eliminate words forever, without even a trace remaining in memory. However, the Bible says words have great power, because they are an extension of our personality. God's Word, especially, always accomplishes his purposes, because it is spoken with his personal power.

In this chapter Paul focuses on the exciting potential of God-inspired speech in the Christian community. Having established in chapter 13 that love should motivate all the gifts, Paul now turns to a concrete example of love-ministry through inspired speech. But like every exciting gift, there are abuses to be understood and regulated, as we shall soon see.

1. Recall a time when something that was shared from the congregation during a worship service (or in a small group) truly encouraged you. What characterized this word ministry?

2. Read 1 Corinthians 14:1-19. Evidently, the Corinthians placed great value on the gift of tongues. Why does Paul prefer prophecy to (uninterpreted) tongues (vv. 1-5)?

3. What illustrations does Paul use to show why (uninterpreted) tongues do not build up the church (vv. 6-12)?

What remedy does Paul suggest (vv. 13-19)?

4. In what ways might we be guilty of meaningless or mindless worship today?

How can Paul's counsel improve the quality of our worship?

5. Read 14:20-25. What does Paul say about the *purpose* of tongues and of prophecy?

Why would prophetic speech rather than tongues cause visitors to sense God in our midst (vv. 23-25)?

6. Read 14:26-40. Based on verse 26 and Paul's statements about the Lord's Supper in 11:17-34, try to describe a typical worship service in Corinth.

7. What guidelines does Paul give for when someone should speak in tongues and when he should remain silent (vv. 27-28)?

8. Under what circumstances should prophets speak or remain silent, and why (vv. 29-33)?

9. What regulations does Paul give women about speaking or remaining silent, and why (vv. 33-35)?

How can Paul's statements here be harmonized with his teaching about women praying and prophesying (11:5)?

10. Some worship services are so "orderly" that they put us to sleep. Others are so "free" that they seem out of control. How does this chapter promote both freedom and order in our worship?

13
Hope in Christ:
The Resurrection and the Life
1 Corinthians 15:1—16:24

What happens after death? Do we live on as disembodied souls, as the Greeks taught? Do we go through countless cycles of reincarnation, as the Hindus believe? Do both body and soul cease to exist, as naturalism maintains?

Because of their Greek heritage, the Corinthians questioned the reality of the resurrection. In this passage Paul challenges their thinking by pointing out the absurd conclusions to which it leads. He reminds us that the resurrection is a crucial aspect of our hope in Christ.

1. How do you react when asked to talk about life after death?

2. Read 1 Corinthians 15:1-11. Paul reminds the Corinthians of the gospel he preached to them. What are the essential elements of the gospel?

What importance does the resurrection of Christ play in Paul's gospel?

3. Read 15:12-28. If there is no resurrection, what are the consequences for

Christ, for Paul and for us (vv. 12-19)?

4. Why is "fallen asleep" (vv. 18, 20) a good way to describe the dead in Christ?

5. How will Christ's resurrection overcome the effects of Adam's sin (vv. 21-29)?

6. Read 15:29-34. How does belief or disbelief in the resurrection affect a person's lifestyle?

7. How can our lifestyle affect our witness to a world bent on "eating and drinking"?

8. Read 15:35-49. What illustrations does Paul use to explain why the resurrection is not illogical but makes good sense (vv. 35-41)?

9. Although the resurrection body is somehow related to the natural body, how is it also radically different (vv. 42-49)?

10. Read 15:50-58. What message is there in these verses for those who grow weary of this physical world and long to escape to heaven?

11. Read chapter 16. How does this chapter give several illustrations of "the work of the Lord" Paul referred to in 15:58?

To which specific area of service will you give yourself this week, knowing that your labor in the Lord is not in vain?

12. What is the most substantial change that studying 1 Corinthians has brought about in your life or group?

Leader's Notes

Leading a Bible discussion can be an enjoyable and rewarding experience. But it can also be *scary*—especially if you've never done it before. If this is your feeling, you're in good company. When God asked Moses to lead the Israelites out of Egypt, he replied, "O Lord, please send someone else to do it!" (Ex 4:13).

When Solomon became king of Israel, he felt the task was far beyond his abilities. "I am only a little child and do not know how to carry out my duties. . . . Who is able to govern this great people of yours?" (1 Kings 3:7, 9).

When God called Jeremiah to be a prophet, he replied, "Ah, Sovereign LORD, . . . I do not know how to speak; I am only a child" (Jer 1:6).

The list goes on. The apostles were "unschooled, ordinary men" (Acts 4:13). Timothy was young, frail and frightened. Paul's "thorn in the flesh" made him feel weak. But God's response to all of his servants—including you—is essentially the same: "My grace is sufficient for you" (2 Cor 12:9). Relax. God helped these people in spite of their weaknesses, and he can help you in spite of your feelings of inadequacy.

There is another reason why you should feel encouraged. Leading a Bible discussion is not difficult if you follow certain guidelines. You don't need to be an expert on the Bible or a trained teacher. The suggestions listed below should enable you to effectively and enjoyably fulfill your role as leader.

Preparing to Lead

1. Ask God to help you understand and apply the passage to your own life. Unless this happens, you will not be prepared to lead others. Pray too for the various members of the group. Ask God to give you an enjoyable and profitable time together studying his Word.

2. As you begin each study, read and reread the assigned Bible passage to familiarize yourself with what the author is saying. In the case of book studies, you may want to read through the entire book prior to the first study. This will give you a helpful overview of its contents.

3. This study guide is based on the New International Version of the Bible. It will help you and the group if you use this translation as the basis for your study and discussion. Encourage others to use the NIV also, but allow them the freedom to use whatever translation they prefer.

4. Carefully work through each question in the study. Spend time in meditation and reflection as you formulate your answers.

5. Write your answers in the space provided in the study guide. This will help you to express your understanding of the passage clearly.

6. It might help you to have a Bible dictionary handy. Use it to look up any unfamiliar words, names or places. (For additional help on how to study a passage, see chapter five of *Leading Bible Discussions*, IVP.)

7. Once you have finished your own study of the passage, familiarize yourself with the leader's notes for the study you are leading. These are designed to help you in several ways. First, they tell you the purpose the study guide author had in mind while writing the study. Take time to think through how the study questions work together to accomplish that purpose. Second, the notes provide you with additional background information or comments on some of the questions. This information can be useful if people have difficulty understanding or answering a question. Third, the leader's notes can alert you to potential problems you may encounter during the study.

8. If you wish to remind yourself of anything mentioned in the leader's notes, make a note to yourself below that question in the study.

Leading the Study

1. Begin the study on time. Unless you are leading an evangelistic Bible study, open with prayer, asking God to help you to understand and apply the passage.

2. Be sure that everyone in your group has a study guide. Encourage them to prepare beforehand for each discussion by working through the questions in the guide.

3. At the beginning of your first time together, explain that these studies are meant to be discussions not lectures. Encourage the members of the group to participate. However, do not put pressure on those who may be hesitant to speak during the first few sessions.

4. Read the introductory paragraph at the beginning of the discussion. This will orient the group to the passage being studied.

5. Read the passage aloud if you are studying one chapter or less. You may choose to do this yourself, or someone else may read if he or she has been asked to do so prior to the study. Longer passages may occasionally be read in parts at different times during the study. Some studies may cover several chapters. In such cases reading aloud would probably take too much time, so the group members should simply read the assigned passages prior to the study.

6. As you begin to ask the questions in the guide, keep several things in mind. First, the questions are designed to be used just as they are written. If you wish, you may simply read them aloud to the group. Or you may prefer to express them in your own words. However, unnecessary rewording of the questions is not recommended.

Second, the questions are intended to guide the group toward understanding and applying the *main idea* of the passage. The author of the guide has stated his or her view of this central idea in the *purpose* of the study in the leader's notes. You should try to understand how the passage expresses this idea and how the study questions work together to lead the group in that direction.

There may be times when it is appropriate to deviate from the study guide. For example, a question may have already been answered. If so, move on to the next question. Or someone may raise an important question not covered in the guide. Take time to discuss it! The important thing is to use discretion. There may be many routes you can travel to reach the goal of the study. But the easiest route is usually the one the author has suggested.

7. Avoid answering your own questions. If necessary, repeat or rephrase them until they are clearly understood. An eager group quickly becomes passive and silent if they think the leader will do most of the talking.

8. Don't be afraid of silence. People may need time to think about the question before formulating their answers.

9. Don't be content with just one answer. Ask, "What do the rest of you think?" or "Anything else?" until several people have given answers to the question.

10. Acknowledge all contributions. Try to be affirming whenever possible. Never reject an answer. If it is clearly wrong, ask, "Which verse led you to that conclusion?" or again, "What do the rest of you think?"

11. Don't expect every answer to be addressed to you, even though this will probably happen at first. As group members become more at ease, they will begin to truly interact with each other. This is one sign of a healthy discussion.

12. Don't be afraid of controversy. It can be very stimulating. If you don't resolve an issue completely, don't be frustrated. Move on and keep it in mind for later. A subsequent study may solve the problem.

13. Stick to the passage under consideration. It should be the source for answering the questions. Discourage the group from unnecessary cross-referencing. Likewise, stick to the subject and avoid going off on tangents.

14. Periodically summarize what the *group* has said about the passage. This helps to draw together the various ideas mentioned and gives continuity to the study. But don't preach.

15. Conclude your time together with conversational prayer. Be sure to ask God's help to apply those things which you learned in the study.

16. End on time.

Many more suggestions and helps are found in *Leading Bible Discussions* (IVP). Reading and studying through that would be well worth your time.

Components of Small Groups

A healthy small group should do more than study the Bible. There are four components you should consider as you structure your time together.

Nurture. Being a part of a small group should be a nurturing and edifying experience. You should grow in your knowledge and love of God and each other. If we are to properly love God, we must know and keep his commandments (Jn 14:15). That is why Bible study should be a foundational part of your small group. But you can be nurtured by other things as well. You can memorize Scripture, read and discuss a book, or occasionally listen to a tape of a good speaker.

Community. Most people have a need for close friendships. Your small group can be an excellent place to cultivate such relationships. Allow time for informal interaction before and after the study. Have a time of sharing during the meeting. Do fun things together as a group, such as a potluck supper or a picnic. Have someone bring refreshments to the meeting. Be creative!

Worship. A portion of your time together can be spent in worship and prayer. Praise

God together for who he is. Thank him for what he has done and is doing in your lives and in the world. Pray for each other's needs. Ask God to help you to apply what you have learned. Sing hymns together.

Mission. Many small groups decide to work together in some form of outreach. This can be a practical way of applying what you have learned. You can host a series of evangelistic discussions for your friends or neighbors. You can visit people at a home for the elderly. Help a widow with cleaning or repair jobs around her home. Such projects can have a transforming influence on your group.

For a detailed discussion of the nature and function of small groups, read *Small Group Leaders' Handbook* or *Good Things Come in Small Groups* (both from IVP).

Study 1. Called in Christ: Saints Made of Clay Not Plaster. 1 Corinthians 1:1-31.

Purpose: To understand the root cause behind quarreling and divisions within Christian groups and churches.

Introduction. Paul begins his letter dealing with first things first. What could be more disruptive than quarreling and divisions in the body? But what surprises us is that Paul couches his treatment of the problem in the context of wisdom. You should beware of identifying this wisdom with the positive Old Testament variety found in Proverbs. Paul isn't attacking wisdom from God but rather the worldly wisdom which leads to boasting, quarreling and factions. He wants to introduce the mature to the true way of wisdom, which leads to humility, unity and a weakness that appears foolish to most.

Question 1. Every study begins with an "approach" question, which is meant to be asked before the passage is read. These questions are important for several reasons. First, they help the group to warm up to each other. No matter how well a group may know each other, there is always a stiffness that needs to be overcome before people will begin to talk openly. A good question will break the ice.

Second, approach questions get people thinking along the lines of the topic of the study. Most people will have lots of different things going on in their minds (dinner, an important meeting coming up, how to get the car fixed) that will have nothing to do with the study. A creative question will get their attention and draw them into the discussion.

Third, approach questions can reveal where our thoughts or feelings need to be transformed by Scripture. This is why it is especially important not to read the passage before the approach question is asked. The passage will tend to color the honest reactions people would otherwise give because they are of course supposed to think the way the Bible does. Giving honest responses to various issues before they find out what the Bible says may help them to see where their thoughts or attitudes need to be changed.

Question 3. Paul was the founder of the church in Corinth and had kept close ties with it. Naturally, many would be loyal to their spiritual father who was obviously a gifted leader.

Apollos was a Jew from Alexandria who became a Christian in Ephesus shortly after

Paul left Corinth. He was sent to Achaia (the Roman province of which Corinth was a chief city) where "he was a great help to those who by grace had believed" (Acts 18:24-28). It is not surprising that some would want to become his followers.

We are not sure if the reference to Cephas (or Peter—both names mean "rock," but in different languages) indicates a visit by Peter to Corinth or simply the presence of believers influenced by him.

The group that claimed to follow Christ probably refers to the most insidious faction of all. Evidently this group felt and acted spiritually superior to the other groups who followed merely human leaders.

Question 5. The transition to Paul's main response to the problems of quarreling and division comes at verse 17. The four key biblical themes introduced in this verse are the gospel, wisdom, the cross of Christ and power. These form the framework for the rest of this chapter and the next three, and play an important role in the whole letter. Don't worry if the group doesn't yet understand these concepts. They will be covered in detail later.

Question 7. Aristides said that on every street in Corinth one met a so-called wise man, who offered his own solutions to the world's problems. The Greeks were intensely interested in philosophic discussions (see Acts 17:21) and often followed their own favorite philosopher. When Paul and his companions came to Corinth, they were viewed within this framework. The Corinthians assumed Paul, Apollos and Cephas were a new kind of wise men and that the gospel was simply a new kind of wisdom. Typically, they aligned themselves with one leader or another and began quarreling over who was the best. Paul attempts to show that they misunderstand both the message and the messengers of the cross, which are considered foolish by the world. Throughout the next three chapters he argues that "the foolishness of God is wiser than man's wisdom, and the weakness of God is stronger than man's strength" (1 Cor 1:25).

Question 8. Pride was the ultimate cause of quarreling and divisions in Corinth. Each group thought it's leader was superior, its teaching most profound and its members most distinguished. Paul shatters this notion by reminding them that they were and are the nobodies of the world. That is why God chose them, not because of their imagined superiority.

Question 10. Help the group to take what they have learned about the sources of disunity and to turn them around into positive principles of community-building: preferring the "foolishness" of God over the "wisdom" of men, remembering our own roots, and boasting in the Lord rather than in his messengers.

Question 11. Encourage the group to explore how Christ has become our wisdom, righteousness, holiness and redemption—as well as our source of pride.

Study 2. Mind of Christ: True Wisdom from the Spirit. 1 Corinthians 2:1—3:4.

Purpose: To learn how we receive and apply the true wisdom we have in Christ.

Question 2. In chapter 2 Paul continues to contrast the wisdom of the world and the wisdom of God. This contrast is seen first in the style of Paul's ministry in Corinth (vv. 1-5, 13). His message did not depend on wise words of the world but on powerful words of the cross. Paul then maintains that the world did not recognize the secret wisdom of God, wisdom that has to do with the power of the crucifixion (vv. 6-9, 14). Finally, he insists that it is only by the Spirit that one can receive and understand the wisdom of God (vv. 10-12, 15-16).

You must be careful not to divorce this chapter from the wider issues of 1 Corinthians. Throughout the epistle Paul hints at the tragedy of tasting the things of the Spirit, as the Corinthians certainly had, and yet still missing out on the true wisdom of God.

Question 3. We must understand verses 1-5 in their historical and cultural context. Compared to the Greek orators of his day, Paul's speaking didn't measure up ("In person he is unimpressive and his speaking amounts to nothing" 2 Cor 10:10). Yet Paul's sermons demonstrated rhetorical power and a sensitive shaping of his message to fit the audience. Further, in his writing—including this epistle to the Corinthians—Paul frequently employed literary devices that would be very much at home in Greek letters of his day ("His letters are weighty and forceful" 2 Cor 10:10). Thus keeping Christ and the cross at the heart of one's message is not at odds with effective communication. Instead, Paul is decrying the empty sophistry of Greek teachers who loved to debate points while paying no regard to the truth. It is possible that some members of the Corinthian church were attracted to such speaking arts; Paul was not.

Question 4. This is a difficult subject. Christians have greatly benefited from advances in printing, radio, television and other modern forms of communication. God has used each of these to spread the gospel and build his church. Yet when do these tools of the world become worldly? Ask the group!

Question 5. The wisdom of this age is available to everyone through investigation, research or experience. But such methods can tell us nothing about God's thoughts and plans. God's wisdom remains absolutely hidden from us unless God chooses to reveal himself to us. Paul claims that God has, in fact, revealed himself by his Spirit.

Verse 9 is a quote from Isaiah 64:1-5. *Mystery* or *secret wisdom* in the New Testament refers to the truths of the gospel, not to some special esoteric knowledge.

Questions 7, 9 & 10. Paul sees all of humanity as divided into those who have the Spirit (Christians) and those who do not (non-Christians). Yet not all those who have the Spirit are "spiritual," as Paul indicates in 3:1-4. A spiritual Christian is a "mature" Christian (2:6) as opposed to an "infant" (3:1). Those who are spiritually mature can eat "solid food" (that is, understand God's wisdom) whereas infants can only drink "milk" (the elementary truths of the gospel). Unfortunately, the Corinthians were neither spiritually mature nor infants. Although they had the Spirit, their spiritual growth had been stunted through disobedience (3:4). Paul calls them "worldly" (3:1)—those whose actions and understanding was infantile even though they had known Christ for a few years.

Question 8. Care is required to avoid concluding that believers are above all forms of judgment from others. In the moral sphere believers are very open to outside criticism and correction, as Paul himself demonstrates in chapters 5 and 6. Yet Paul knows that a life lived through and for the gospel will not always be understood by those without the Spirit.

Study 3. Founded on Christ: Indwelt by the Spirit. 1 Corinthians 3:5-23.

Purpose: To discover how the church is like a field being planted, a building under construction and a temple indwelt by God.

Question 2. The group may have difficulty with this question at first. Help them to see that Paul compares himself and Apollos to farmers (vv. 6-9) and builders (vv. 10-15). He likewise compares the church to God's field (v. 9), God's building (v. 9) and God's temple (v. 16). Don't worry about the details of these metaphors at this point, since they will be covered later in the study.

Question 3. In the first part of this question, be sure to look not only at the field but also at the workers in the field.

Question 4. Notice that there is a master builder (Paul), a foundation (Jesus Christ), building materials (gold, silver, wood), other builders (ministers like Apollos and Cephas) and a day when the owner of the building will judge the quality of the construction.

Question 6. Using an image that spans the centuries, Paul pictures a fire raging through a city, hardly touching masonary buildings but consuming wooden and grass shacks, with the builder of such flimsy structures barely escaping "like a man pulled to safety through the smoke and flames of his burning house" (F. F. Bruce, *1 and 2 Corinthians* [London: Marshall, Morgan and Scott, 1978], p. 44).

The image of fiery judgment may cause some Christians to question their salvation because they are so aware of being poor witnesses or of having failed in some Christian service. But the builder's salvation is not in question, for that is by God's grace, but rather the "reward" (vv. 8, 14) of having built something of lasting value that will survive God's judgment.

Question 7. Paul is thinking primarily of building the Christian community. But throughout his letters Paul teaches that our calling embraces all of life. Vocation is not only the work of the ministry but the ministry of work! It is not only building the house of God, but building one's family for God. Whether we work for God in so-called secular society or in the Christian community, we serve the same God for the same reason with the same motivation.

Question 8. Throughout 1 Corinthians it is amazing to observe that God's salvation, presence and gifts are not dependent on our maturity or obedience but rather on his grace.

Question 9. People often assume that Paul is speaking of destroying the temple of our bodies through such things as smoking, drinking and so on. But the temple Paul refers to here is not our bodies (as in 1 Cor 6:19) but the church as a whole. Likewise, the destruction he has in mind is not individual but corporate.

The church as God's building, built on "the stone" (Is 28:16), is not something we break; we break ourselves against it. As a Pharisee persecuting the church, Paul himself had found that it is hard "to kick against the goads" (Acts 26:14) and he will soon mention how some community-destroying persons in Corinth had hurt themselves by failing to discern their relationships within the body of Christ (1 Cor 11:30). **Question 10.** God has given us everything in Christ. Unfortunately, the NIV obscures the parallel between 1:12 and 3:21-23 by the translation "I *follow* Paul" rather than "I *belong to* Paul" (RSV), which is implied by the Greek. The idea of belonging (as well as union) is also implied by the statements "You are of Christ, and Christ is of God" (3:23).

The ground is level before the cross. No matter what our background, education, income or position in the church, we are all simply servants of God. The world calls this holy egalitarianism foolishness, too, but it is God's wisdom in community-building.

Study 4. Servants of Christ: At the End of the Procession. 1 Corinthians 4:1-21.

Purpose: To challenge people to become fools for Christ.

Introduction. There are a lot of themes in this chapter which tie together the previous three. Here one gets the clearest picture of what it means to be a fool for Christ. The paragraph is rich in irony—the use of words to express something other than the literal meaning, usually pointing to an incongruity between observation and reality. There is the irony that the Corinthians believe they have become spiritual kings; the irony that Paul and the other apostles most deserving of honor are in fact the scum of the earth; finally, the irony that being a sacrificial servant of Christ and his gospel may cause us to be viewed as fools in the eyes of the world (and even of arrogant segments of the church) but will one day lead to glory.

Everyone in the study should go away feeling the weight of this truth: having died on the cross with Christ, we must now bear our cross in ministry to others. We must be fools with eyes fixed on eternal glory.

Question 2. The first part of this question is fairly easy to answer, so don't dwell on it. The second part requires more thought.

Question 3. Christians today often make the same mistakes as the Corinthians. We judge on the basis of appearance, personality, speaking ability, prestige, success and so on.

Paul is unconcerned about the judgment of others, whether those in the world or in the church, and he is hesitant to judge himself. Yet some qualifications are immediately necessary.

First, Paul is not declaring himself perfect. Verse 4 may be translated "I am conscious of nothing against myself, yet I am not by this acquitted" (NASB). He simply does not feel he or anyone else is qualified to judge in this particular circumstance.

Second, the circumstance is *specific.* Paul is not saying he is above the assessment of the community or of introspection when it comes to moral issues. The question here is not morality but rather the manner and motive of ministry. In this regard Paul is adamant—only the Lord is capable of judging motives and giving rewards. With an eye fixed on eternal judgment, Paul's only concern is to be a faithful servant.

Question 4. The mention of Apollos here and again (perhaps with frustration) in 16:12, and the absence of any evidence that Cephas (Peter) actually visited Corinth, makes it likely that the Apollos party was in fact Paul's main source of grief. These were folks who had forgotten that all leaders were given to them as a gift from God (see 3:22). Therefore, it was highly inappropriate to elevate one over the other. Even more, the style and content of wisdom which they may have prized in Apollos was either worldly or quite possibly a gift of God. In either case it was no ground for boasting in men. It is good to know that Titus 3:13 suggests a happy ending in the relationship between Paul and Apollos.

Question 5. Scripture teaches this, for example, in Romans 8:17-39. Paul's words only make sense in light of this concept of suffering before glory. For example, the Bible teaches that having suffered, Christ now reigns in glory (Col 3:1). We too will reign with him in glory at his return (Col 3:4) provided we share in his sufferings now (Rom 8:17).

The Corinthians, however, wanted to have the glory now and skip the suffering. Or, perhaps more accurately, they assumed that suffering was a sign of weakness and a lack of God's blessing. Therefore, they had no alternative but to conclude that Paul must be a poor example of a Christian. Paul stands this kind of thinking on its head!

As the group contrasts the Corinthians' experiences with those of Paul and the apostles, be sure to notice the vivid language Paul uses. The group should try to imagine what Paul is describing. He is thinking of the gladiatorial contests in the Roman arena, or perhaps the triumphal procession of a Roman general. The Christians are on display at the end of the procession and are brought in to the arena to die. The whole universe, including the angels, are in the stands watching this spectacle.

The deepest irony in this paragraph is that the Corinthians have not yet learned that the only way to the front of the procession is to serve at the end of it. Thus they may appear wise next to Paul. They may think themselves superior. But in the end the foolish apostle, condemned to die, is the one on the royal road. Of course, this is the same road that his Lord walked before him; and note (especially in v. 12) that it is the kind of road mapped out in the Sermon on the Mount.

Question 8. The group should answer this question first with regard to the Corinthians and then with regard to their own thoughts and actions.

Questions 9-10. Paul may be referring to ecstatic speech and other signs and wonders. However, in light of the first four chapters, this seems unlikely (see, for example, 1:22). It is much more likely that Paul is thinking in 4:20 of the power of the cross as a sign of the kingdom—a power made evident in the sacrificial servanthood of his ministry.

Thus a whip is not the necessary symbol of power. Paul knows that a spirit of love and humility can break the stoniest of hearts. For it is when one comes in weakness and fear and trembling that God's power is revealed (2:3, 5). This is the kind of "wise folly" that the Corinthians needed to learn (3:18). As Paul wrote them in a later epistle: "That is why, for Christ's sake, I delight in weaknesses, in insults, in hardships, in persecutions, in difficulties. For when I am weak, then I am strong" (2 Cor 12:10).

Study 5. Members of Christ: The Body Is Meant for the Lord. 1 Corinthians 5:1—6:20.

Purpose: To grasp the importance of corporate and personal purity.

Question 2. The NIV uses the words "sexual immorality" (v. 1) for the Greek *porneia. Porneia* is a general word for unlawful sexual behavior ranging from sexual relationships before marriage to sexual relationships outside of marriage. One of the few Old Testament regulations imposed on gentile Christians, who lacked a Jewish moral and religious heritage, was this ban on fornication (Acts 15:29; 21:25). It has been said that the one virtue that the church gave to the ancient world was chastity.

That a man should cohabit with his stepmother, even though she be younger than he, was forbidden by Old Testament law (Lev 18:8; Deut 22:30; 27:20). Old Testament examples of such outrageous fornication are found in Genesis 35:22; 49:4; 1 Chronicles 5:1; 2 Samuel 16:22; 20:3.

Question 3. Handing this person "over to Satan" probably means to expel him from the community where Jesus is confessed as Lord into the secular realm where Satan dominates (1 Tim 1:20; Mt 18:17-19). But Paul adds the important qualifying purpose: "That the sinful nature [*sarx* or "flesh"] may be destroyed and his spirit saved on the day of the Lord" (v. 5). Either Paul is prophesying a physical sickness as God's disciplinary punishment of this man (as in 11:30) or he is intending that exclusion from the Christian community would result, eventually, in repentance (crucifying the sinful nature) and true spiritual life before God. In either case Paul's desire is that the person be saved, not damned.

Many people have heard or experienced examples of disastrous and usually unwarranted church discipline. In reaction they want no part in church discipline and would rather tolerate a gross sin than to risk losing the offender. It will be important to guide people to notice how Paul disciplines the church and, only indirectly, the individual. A living church requires tough love.

Question 4. The Passover and the Feast of Unleavened Bread which followed it were an annual remembrance of Israel's miraculous deliverance from Egypt (Ex 12). During this festival all the old leaven was removed from the house in order to make a clean start and to remember the unleavened bread they made while escaping from Egypt.

According to John's Gospel Jesus was crucified while the Passover lambs were being slain, a powerful statement of the New Exodus he accomplished. Paul implies that the Passover lamb has been slain for the Corinthians, but God's house (the Christian community) has not been cleansed of the old yeast of malice and wickedness (v. 8). Objective salvation requires subjective cleansing.

Question 5. The Corinthians practiced an odd kind of separation. Ironically, they tolerated gross sin within their fellowship while having as little possible contact with sinners outside the church! Paul shows that freedom in Christ gives one the courage to deal with sin *within* the community while having genuine relationships with people *outside* the community—yet without conforming to their lifestyle.

Question 6. "We will judge angels" (v. 3) may refer to the fact that those associated with the Son of Man (Jesus) will share his ultimate reign over the earth (Dan 7:22). Or it could refer to our share in Christ's victory over even disobedient angels (Jude 6)—or both. Christians can hardly be fitting to share Christ's rule and judgment if they resort to pagans to settle their disputes.

Commenting on Paul's restatement of the principle of nonretaliation taught by Jesus (Mt 5:39-42), T. W. Manson suggests that Paul is making two points: first, that Christian cases should be tried by Christian courts and, second, that there should be no cases! *(Studies in the Gospels and Epistles* [Manchester University Press, 1962], p. 198.)

Question 7. Paul warns us against being deceived because we *are* so easily deceived about this. After all, salvation is by grace, not by works, and Jesus came to save sinners. What does it matter (we think) if sinners keep on sinning? But such thinking overlooks the fact that a new life in Christ results in a new lifestyle (v. 11).

The sins listed refer to a continuous lifestyle or practice and not to a one-time involvement. Paul's list is similar to the works of the flesh in Galatians 5:19-21. (See also Ephesians 5:5.) In both cases a persisting in fleshly living is implied.

Likewise, Paul's mention of both "male prostitutes" and "homosexual offenders" does not mean that a person with a homosexual tendency who is living chastely is excluded from the kingdom. The two words Paul uses here, *malakoi* (men or boys who allow themselves to be misused homosexually) and *arsenokoitai* (a male homosexual, pederast, sodomite) both have an active meaning.

Question 9. There is a vast difference between those who are seeking to overcome their sin and those who embrace it and refuse to repent. The former description would apply to every Christian, whereas the latter would apply to those whom Paul would put out of the church.

What about the fact that Paul called the Corinthians "worldly" and immature (3:1)? Why not put them out of the church as well? It is true that Paul used these words to describe the Corinthians, but that was because of their pride, quarreling and inability to understand the "solid food" in God's Word. However, we must balance this description with Paul's claim that the Corinthians no longer lived as they did as non-Christians (6:11). They still had a long way to go, but they had changed in many ways. Unfortunately, people today often apply the label of "worldly" or "carnal" Christian to those whom Paul would not consider Christians at all.

Question 10. Paul uses a number of arguments to refute the idea that "everything is permissible for me":

1. He states that although everything is permissible, not everything is beneficial (v. 12).

2. In contrast to the Greek idea that the body is the prison of the soul, Paul claims that God will resurrect our bodies just as he raised Jesus from the dead (v. 14).

3. He emphasizes that our bodies are members of Christ and should be treated accordingly (vv. 15-17).

4. In contrast to other sins, Paul claims that sexual sins are committed against our own bodies (v. 18).

5. Paul states that our bodies are temples of the Holy Spirit and should be treated as holy (v. 19).

6. He stresses that our bodies are not our own but have been purchased by God and belong to him (v. 20).

Separately and together these provide powerful reasons for honoring God with our bodies (v. 20).

Study 6. Devoted to Christ: Marrying When Time Is Short. 1 Corinthians 7:1-40.

Purpose: To discover how our devotion to Christ should affect our views of singleness, sex and marriage.

Introduction. Paul does not give us in this chapter a complete theology or handbook of marriage. He is dealing with specific issues through which we must "mine" timeless truths. Genesis 1:26-28 and 2:18-25 speak about the companionship function of marriage, and in Ephesians 5:21-33 Paul develops the mysterious parallel of husband/wife and Christ/church. Look in this chapter for what Paul teaches, not for what he omits.

Question 2. "It is good for a man not to marry" (v. 1 NIV) is not in quotation marks like "all things are lawful" (6:12). Some commentators feel it is a quote from a letter delivered to Paul from Corinth, rather than Paul's inspired word. Others believe it is Paul's own statement on the subject. In either case, Paul doesn't refute the statement but rather discusses why it may not be "good" for most people to refrain from marriage.

Different translations may confuse the exact issue Paul is addressing. The RSV and KJV follow the original Greek literally by saying "not to touch a woman." The NIV translates this "not to marry" because the exact meaning of the word is to touch in sexual intercourse (see Prov 6:29). Some feel that Paul considers the matter from the male point of view ("have no physical contact with women" Phillips), but we will soon discover how Paul was equally concerned for the purity, health and fulfillment of women, a remarkable thing in his own day.

Paul's use of *gift* (v. 7) may lead to significant confusion. Some may think that celibacy (the single life) is a special capacity given by God (like a "gift of teaching") that makes it easy to be single. But in Paul's correspondence, *gift* is literally a *gracelet,* a favor freely bestowed by God (Arndt and Gingrich, *Greek-English Lexicon,* p. 887). Being able to remain contentedly single is not the result of having little desire or capacity for marriage (though Jesus alluded to *this* in Matthew 19:11-12). As Paul understands it, remaining contentedly single or contentedly married both require *grace.* Here, as elsewhere, devotion to Christ overrides what is natural or easy.

Question 3. In verse 2 Paul mentions that "there is so much immorality." At one time there were over 1,000 sacred prostitutes in the temple to Aphrodite (goddess of love) in Corinth. However, the sexual attitudes and temptations in Corinth were not much different than those people face today.

Paul's practical advice that "each man should have his own wife, and each woman her own husband" (v. 2) may not seem so practical to those who would like to get married but, for whatever reason, cannot. If there are singles in your group, you may wish to discuss what Paul does not cover here: How can singles who do not have Paul's "gift" avoid sexual immorality if they have no immediate prospects for marriage?

Question 4. Using the word *duty* (v. 3) Paul describes marital obligations the same way he does the obligation to pay taxes (Rom 13:7)! In verse 4 he also uses the Greek word for "authority" or "right" *(exousia)* to describe the right or power each spouse has over the other's body. However, Paul's emphasis is on a radical self-giving rather than a selfish spouse-taking.

Some may be offended at this seeming sexual imperialism. But it is important to note that sexual submission in this chapter is *mutual:* the wife has equal rights to her husband's body, just as the husband has rights to his wife's body.

Questions 5. Many groups today have someone who is separated or divorced. Almost every group has children of divorced parents. Pastoral sensitivity is needed in approaching these questions without compromising Scripture. A compassionate heart is the key to accepting people who have broken God's Word or who are victims of a fallen world.

Paul quotes the words of the Lord Jesus, referring probably to Mark 10:2-12, especially the statement, "what God has joined together let not man separate" (v. 9). Jesus used the same word "separate" or "leave" *(chorizeto)* that Paul chose in 1 Corinthians 7:10, 15a and 15b.

Many think this passage teaches two options for a seemingly hopeless marriage: separation of bed and board (without divorce), and divorce. But the Bible does not envisage a separation that is not a divorce. If there is no intercourse, no living together (v. 12), there is no marriage. However, the corollary: that two people who have slept together are married is not what Paul teaches either.

When Paul writes in verse 11, "A husband must not divorce *[aphienai]* his wife," he uses another word, *aphieme,* which means to "send away in the legal sense of divorce" or "to dismiss one's spouse." Jewish society regulated very liberally the rights of a husband to divorce his wife. Some rabbis interpreted Deuteronomy 24:1 to mean that a man could divorce his wife if he now found her unattractive! But the Jewish woman could not divorce her husband, a right which Roman custom gave also to the woman. Jesus and Paul took that "right" away in favor of a higher right, the power and possibility of living for God in the place of life you are in when God calls you (vv. 17, 20).

Paul's statement "but if she does" (v. 11) considers the possibility that a (presumably believing) woman might take the initiative to separate and divorce. In this case she is not "free" to remarry because she has broken the marriage covenant. She must remain unmarried or be reconciled.

Question 7. The biblical "grounds" for permissible divorce make for hot discussion. The evangelical consensus is that there are two permissible grounds for divorce which give the right to remarry: adultery by one's partner (not oneself), and the desertion of the unbelieving spouse. However, in spite of a general consensus, many evangelicals hold a variety of views on divorce and remarriage, including the following:

1. Divorce is not allowed under any circumstances.

2. Divorce is allowed for sexual immorality or desertion of an unbelieving partner, but remarriage is not permitted.

3. Divorce and remarriage are allowed for sexual immorality or desertion of an unbelieving partner.

4. Divorce and remarriage are allowed for a variety of reasons.

Obviously it is not possible for the group to research all of the relevant passages in this study. It is important, therefore, to focus on Paul's concerns in *this* passage rather than trying to answer more questions than he is addressing.

Realize, too, that Paul's concern was not to regulate permissible divorce but to maintain healthy spirituality in believers, even in a mixed marriage. Since groups tend to focus on the rules of divorce it will be important to stay with the concern of the text: being devoted to the Lord whether married or single, whether "happily" married or not.

Question 10. These verses are some of the most difficult in the chapter partly because of confusing translations. The NIV accurately communicates that *called* in verses 17 and 20 is used in *two senses:* First, God has sovereignly assigned a place for us. Our life is not a series of accidents. Paul emphasizes this in verse 17: "Each one should retain the place in life that the Lord assigned to him and *to which God has called him.*" But this is not Paul's main use of *called.*

Second, in verse 20 he emphasizes that God's call to live in the kingdom of God (Eph 4:1; 1 Cor 1:26) comes to us *where we are:* "Each one should remain in the situation which he was in *when* God called him" (v. 20).

Both senses are needed to complete our understanding of Christian vocation (the word *vocation* simply means "calling"). God's call makes us be who we are where we are. God's call also evokes kingdom living no matter who we are or where we are. "Never allow the thought—'I am of no use where I am'; because you certainly can be of no use where you are not" (Oswald Chambers, *My Utmost for His Highest* [New York: Dodd, Mead and Co., 1956], p. 291).

Question 11. Paul has already affirmed the holiness of married life and the marriage bed. He has emphasized the spiritual influence a believer may have with an unbelieving partner (vv. 14, 16). Now by emphasizing the advantages of the single life he shows that the single person lacks nothing in being a complete Christian. Sexual fulfillment is not necessary. Your group may wish to discuss the appropriateness of celebrating someone's decision to remain single just as we now celebrate the announcement of someone's engagement!

"Virgins" *(parthenoi,* v. 25) probably refers to a special class of unmarried women, to be distinguished from unmarried women in general *(agamos).* The issue may have been whether women who were betrothed virgins should proceed to marriage in the normal way just because they were pledged to someone. In this chapter, however, Paul has *both* male and female celibacy in mind.

It is frequently argued that Paul's teaching in this chapter (especially verses 25-35) was determined by "this present crisis" (v. 26) and therefore does not apply to all times and all situations. However, Paul offers some powerful reasons for radical devotion to Christ *besides* the "crisis" he refers to (however this is interpreted). He says, for example, that "this world in its present form is passing away" (7:31), which emphasizes the transitoriness of everything secular in comparison with the certainty of Christ's kingdom. He says that married couples will have "troubles in this life" (7:28), and he wants to spare us this. He says that a married couple's interests are divided (v. 34), while he would like us to have undivided devotion to the Lord (v. 35). For Paul, and for those who follow his teaching, it is not life now that sets the agenda but the kingdom and the King.

Question 12. Full covenant marriage in Genesis 2:24 requires three kinds of unity: "leaving" (public wedlock), "cleaving" (personal friendship) and "one flesh" (private consummation). Physical desire alone is an insufficient reason to be married. However, the high incidence of premarital sex in our society, even among Christians, calls for sensitive pastoral ministry. Many Christians hurry up their wedding because they are not able (or willing) to exercise self-control physically. Couples too involved physically have two better choices than a quick wedding: they can abstain physically for a time and work on other levels of intimacy, or they can rely on the judgment of mature and experienced outsiders about their marriageability, and as a result of such counseling either to break off or get married.

Study 7. Living for Christ: The Right to Relinquish Rights. 1 Corinthians 8:1—9:27.

Purpose: To understand that living the gospel is more important than personal rights or even religious principles.

Question 2. There are at least two reasons why the issue of meat sacrificed to idols emerged at this point. First, the Corinthians may have had an uneasy conscience about whether animals slaughtered in pagan worship before idols became spiritually contaminated. They may also have wondered whether Christians should pursue independent butchering and meat preparation, as the Jews did. Second, some in Corinth may have sought to apply the injunction of the Jerusalem council to "abstain from food polluted by idols" and "from the meat of strangled animals and from blood" (Acts 15:20).

Similarly, there are two reasons why the mature would be quite willing to eat idol meat. First, on the pragmatic side, much of the best meat available in the marketplace came straight from the many Corinthian temples, since only a token portion would be "received" by the deity and the surplus could not be consumed by the priests and attendants alone. Second, on the spiritual side, the mature knew that neither idols nor rules about eating idol meat had any meaning next to the true God.

Question 3. Paul cautions the Corinthians against wounding another's conscience by their exercise of rights and freedoms. After all, a brother is of much greater value than food—greater even than our "rights." In particular, Paul has no patience with those who would push freedom beyond the marketplace and into the realm of accepting invitations to dinner parties often held in temples, under the nominal patronage of a pagan deity. Although meaningless to the one "with knowledge" (see 10:18-22), such behavior would have been scandalous to many of the Christians with scruples sensitized by past pagan experience (v. 7). Ultimately, Paul raises the stakes even higher, indicating that love for one's brother is very much connected with one's relationship to God (v. 3) and love for Christ (v. 12).

Question 5. The comments on Paul's apostleship are very much in keeping with the topic of rights and freedoms as outlined in chapter 8. Paul spends the first half of the chapter establishing his apostolic rights. In the second half he explains why he does not claim any of his rights.

It is not exactly clear what lay behind the Corinthians' criticism of Paul's apostolic behavior. They may have felt that Paul's refusal to accept financial support from the church made him suspect. His refusal may have embarrassed the Corinthians, who wanted to be seen as able to provide for their leaders. Perhaps it caused Paul's position of authority to appear weaker than that of his rivals who, one assumes, were not reluctant to receive gifts.

Questions 6-7. One of the first things people criticize about radio and TV preachers, for example, is their constant pleas for money. Unfortunately, such pleas make it easy for people to assume that the preacher is just trying to get rich.

Paul more than once demonstrated a willingness to engage in "holy compromise" for the sake of the gospel (Acts 15:22; 16:3; Gal 2:11-14). In the immediate context, Paul is willing to be "weak" by not eating idol meat if it upsets certain brothers and "strong" against those who would take their freedom too far by eating in idol temples.

In all things Paul's guiding principle is to be a slave to Christ, to the gospel, and to those who need to hear it, not letting any disputable matter stand in the way (see Rom 14). Obviously, such a view requires us to distinguish the heart of the gospel from peripheral issues. Paul has given us some provocative guidelines to make such decisions in a way that is calculated to upset many "sacred cows" in our traditional doctrines and methods of ministry.

Question 8. Paul says that he cannot boast for preaching the gospel, because that is required of him (vv. 16-17). But he can "boast" (v. 15) if he does something beyond what is required, namely to preach free of charge. This is what he has voluntarily chosen to do, and he will be rewarded accordingly.

Question 12. If you have time, you might ask the group what kind of "crown" and "prize" they think Paul expected to receive. Obviously, this provided strong motivation for Paul to give up his rights in order to preach the gospel more effectively. Likewise, it can powerfully motivate us.

Study 8. Eating with Christ: All for the Glory of God. 1 Corinthians 10:1-33.

Purpose: To invite people to choose a life of freedom in Christ that is beneficial for themselves and others.

Questions 2-3. Paul sees parallels between Israel's spiritual experiences and those of the Corinthians. The Israelites were baptized *in* the cloud and sea and *into* (the leadership of) Moses, just as the Corinthians were baptized *in* water and *into* Jesus

Christ. Paul's main point is that both groups were baptized, not *how* they were baptized.

Likewise, the Israelites ate spiritual food (manna) and drank (water from the rock), just as the Corinthians ate the bread and drank the wine during the celebration of holy communion.

However, Israel's spiritual experiences were no guarantee of protection against God's judgment. In spite of their experiences, God judged them because of their idolatry, sexual immorality, testing and grumbling. Likewise, the Corinthians (and we) should beware of sinning against the Lord lest God's judgment fall on them.

These questions may be confusing to members of the group who have very little understanding of the story of Israel's salvation and its significance as a parable of the believer's experience today. The leader should become familiar with these major events by reading about the golden calf (Ex 32:4-6) and the seduction of Israel by Moab (Num 25:1-9).

Paul's reference to drinking out of a rock, as a foretaste of knowing Christ, restates the story of Numbers 20:1-12. The "snakes" (v. 9) were a response to grumbling (Num 21:4-7), the raised bronze snake being a focus for healing faith, though Jesus, not Paul, makes this connection (Jn 3:14).

While few in the group will be able to systematize these wilderness experiences, all can profit from Paul's terse summary of their *meaning:* "These things occurred as examples to keep us from setting our hearts on evil things as they did." Make sure the group understands the intent of Paul's comparison. Just as the whole Israelite nation enjoyed God's blessing at the beginning of the journey, but only a few remained in these blessings, so it is possible that not all redeemed members of the Corinthian community will in the end enjoy Christ's blessing.

As this passage does *not* deal with whether one can lose salvation, it may prove unprofitable to explore this subject here.

Questions 4-5. The Greek word for *temptation* means either a "trial" or "testing." Trials can come from God to produce maturity, just as temptations can come from Satan to make people fall. In these verses both meanings apply. God wanted the pressures of the surrounding pagan culture to be a means of spiritual growth, but Satan used these pressures to seduce believers into sin.

Since God is ultimately in charge and marvelously available (v. 13), the Corinthians have an escape. Make sure the group discovers that the escape is not *from* temptation but *in* it, through overcoming it in Christ's power.

Someone in the group may be able to illustrate how God turned a situation in which Satan seduced toward sin into a trial that produced faith and righteousness. You also need to be sensitive to persons who feel persistent failure before a repeated temptation, or who unwisely put themselves into seductive situations that could never be positive trials. Most will easily think of sexual testings and temptations. It may be more useful and challenging to explore the temptations of greed and pride.

Question 6. The reference to participating in a fellowship table with demons (v. 21) may spark some lively discussion. Paul's argument is very delicate. On the one hand,

Paul sides with the "strong" in saying that an idol is no god at all and has no demonic influence (8:4-7). On the other hand, Paul realizes that the "weak" Christian feels the idol has a real existence and power. Therefore he also lovingly sides with the weak, warning of the danger of unwittingly yielding to the powers of darkness by trying to mix Christian and pagan worship or lifestyle.

The church fathers usually understood this passage to suggest that pagan worshipers sacrificed to particular demons. Some may wish to conclude from this that any involvement in Eastern religion today leads to demon possession. This, however, is more than Paul says. His concern is not to explain pagan idolatry but to win people to undivided participation in the life of Christ in the Spirit.

Question 7. Where the "rubber meets the road" on the doctrine of the Lord's Supper is not whether it is a sacrament or symbol but whether the worshiper truly participates in the death and resurrection of Christ. The person who has a "high" doctrine of the sacrament but lives immorally is practicing a heresy! Stay with what the text says. The table is a "participation" in the blood and body. The Greek word *koinonia* means "fellowship" and shared experience. Paul means no more or less!

Question 8. Once again Paul emphasizes that our "freedom" or our "rights" should not be our primary concern. Rather, he stresses that the following principles should guide our behavior:

1. Do only those things which are beneficial and constructive for yourself and others (v. 23).

2. Don't seek your own good (only), but the good of others (v. 24).

3. Realize that the earth is the Lord's and everything in it—including those things which some people consider spiritually contaminated or inherently evil (such as meat offered to idols, v. 26).

4. Don't do anything that will cause someone's conscience to condemn your freedom in Christ (vv. 28-30).

5. Don't do anything that will cause either non-Christians or Christians to "stumble" (v. 32).

6. Do everything for the glory of God (v. 31).

Paul's argument about food "sold in the meat market" is complicated. Here are the salient points: (1) Paul restates the principle that even if meat has been dedicated to an idol, it can be made *kosher* simply by giving thanks to God (v. 30); (2) while Paul forbids table-fellowship with immoral church members (5:9-12), he does not discourage believers from having table-fellowship with unbelievers, even though the Christians' consciences will be tested on such occasions. Paul's attitude here contrasts sharply with the strict Jewish attitude illustrated by Peter's words to Cornelius (Acts 10:28). (3) Paul seems to have in mind the situation where a pagan might say, "This has been offered in sacrifice" (v. 28) to embarrass the Christian, knowing that idolatry was offensive. During the persecutions of the Jews under Antiochus IV (2 Mac 6:7-11) refusing forbidden food was used as a test of faith. Similar "test cases" presented themselves to Christians in the Roman Empire. In such cases, Paul urged believers to refuse the food, not because it was sinful but in order to bear witness *according to the conscience of the host.*

Question 9. Encourage members of the group to share their own "freedoms" which might cause someone else to stumble. In eastern cultures (and missionary contexts) this is a day-by-day issue. In Western cultures, the principle finds application in less religious matters. Note that Paul's concern is not merely to keep everybody happy by conforming to the expectations of others. He is concerned not to offend the *conscience* of others and hinder their salvation, growth and discipleship. While Paul does not say so directly in this passage, he has a mission to the "strong" to make them more loving, and a mission to the "weak" to make them stronger!

Study 9. Headship of Christ: We Are Interdependent. 1 Corinthians 11:1-34.
Purpose: To discover how we can honor God rather than dishonor him during our worship.

Question 1. The purpose of this question is not to get a "right" answer but to establish a context for the study. People's responses will vary, but the study will challenge everyone to see that we are not independent but interdependent when we worship.

Question 2. It is important to let people share the various possible answers to this question: the relationship between the sexes, authority, order and freedom, and the marriage relationship. All of these answers will give some clue to the passage and help a corporate interpretation to emerge later.

Question 3. Verse 3 is the center of a raging controversy. Those who believe that men should be in authority over women usually interpret *head* as "chief" or "ruler." Likewise, Christian feminists usually interpret it as "source" or "origin."

Some interpreters see a straight hierarchy in verse 3: God is over Christ, who is over man, who is over woman. For a good presentation of this view see James Hurley, *Man and Woman in Biblical Perspective* (Grand Rapids: Zondervan, 1981), p. 166.

However, it may be better to see verse 3 as a series of comparisons. Paul is not emphasizing "God over Christ over man over woman" but rather is saying that the Christ-man relationship is like the man-woman relationship, which is like the God-Christ relationship.

Comparing husband and wife with God the Father and Christ helps us understand headship as a priority within a relationship of equals. It has nothing to do with greater and inferior. The Father has priority over the Son, but they are equal and one (Jn 10:30).

In this series of headship comparisons one common element is the matter of giving glory: the Father is glorified in the Son. Christ glorifies himself in his bride, the church. There is a special sense in which the wife brings glory to her husband by recognizing his place in her life (11:7).

Don't let the group discussion grind to a halt on verse 3—there is more to come! (A mediating position between headship as rule and no headship at all in Christian marriage is taken in R. Paul Stevens, *Married for Good* [Downers Grove, Ill.: InterVarsity Press, 1986], pp. 111-131.)

Question 5. Since we have no cultural equivalent to veils to signal a right marital relationship, we can only imagine the confusion that would result in our own culture if men and women took off their wedding rings in church because some people said, "In Christ sexual differences mean nothing."

Paul's statement "because of the angels" (v. 10) has been interpreted various ways. The most probable is that angels were considered guardians of the created order. Once again Paul feels it is essential to live with the tension of accepting both the way we were created, male and female, *and* the way we are redeemed to be interdependent and equal. Paul also argues from public propriety (v. 13) from nature (v. 14) and from general church practice (v. 16).

In Greek culture, prostitutes and women convicted of adultery often had their heads shaved (see vv. 5-6).

Question 6. Against the background of Genesis 1:26-27 ("In the image of God he created him; male and female he created them"), Paul cannot mean that only males reflect God. He carefully does *not* say that woman is man's "image and likeness." But he does say that a woman will be the "glory" of her husband when she stands in right relationship to him, which is Paul's concern in Corinth. James Hurley, who holds the view that the word *head* means "authority over," comments on this with considerable insight:

> Man, in his authority relation to creation and to his wife, images the dominion of God over the creation (a central theme in Gn. 1) and the headship of Christ over his church (Eph. 1:20-22; 5:22-23, etc.). The woman is not called to image God or Christ *in the relation which she sustains to her husband.* She images instead the response of the church to God and Christ by willing, loving self-subjection (Eph. 5:22-23). In *this particular sense* of authority relationship, the main topic of 1 Corinthians 11, it is absolutely appropriate to say that the man images God and that the woman does not. I want to stress that in saying this there need be no implication whatsoever that women are not the image of God in *other senses.* Paul did not say that man was the image of God and that the woman was the image of the man (*Man and Woman,* p. 173).

Question 8. There are many possible frustrations in this study: How does a single woman or man signal right relationships with the other sex? What exactly is masculinity and femininity? Does God want us to uphold hurtful cultural stereotypes of male or female roles for the presumed good of fighting the tide towards androgyny? Some progress can be made by asking the group what *they* understand about the distinctiveness of each sex and how they have come to celebrate the contribution of both sexes to the body of Christ.

Question 10. The words *fallen asleep* (v. 30) are a euphemism for death. As a result of taking the Lord's Supper in an unworthy manner, God's judgment had fallen on various members of the Corinthian community. This judgment had resulted in weakness, sickness and, in some cases, even death.

The threat of judgment has kept many sensitive believers from receiving the benefits of the Lord's Supper. They simply do not feel good enough! Ironically they are the very people *worthy* to come, if they cling to Christ and his mercy. In contrast, the self-righteous with broken relationships do not take the trouble to examine themselves in the right way and condemn themselves with grace.

Study 10. Body of Christ: Manifestations of the Spirit. 1 Corinthians 12:1-31.

Purpose: To discover the nature and purpose of spiritual gifts.

Question 1. The question is worded so that whether persons in the group are Christians or not they may reflect on the feeling of being prized. Spiritual gifts are not entirely unrelated to natural abilities or talents and may sometimes be an extra anointing of a so-called talent (Rom. 2:6-8). Every good thing comes from God. This may help members of the group include persons in the discussion who are not yet believers or who are confused about spiritual gifts.

Question 2. Paul is once again answering the Corinthians' questions. Paul does not repeat their question, but it may have been: "Which spiritual gift is the most inspired?" or "What is the surest sign of the Holy Spirit?" In replying, Paul is well aware that both tongues (glossalalia—utterance in languages not normally used by the speaker) and prophecy were found in pagan religions. The priestess of Delphi or the fortunetelling slave girl of Acts 16:16 could have been cited. Paul does not attribute any of the gift-ministries in Corinth to demonic or pagan sources, but he does affirm that ecstasy is not the mark of the presence of the Holy Spirit. At this early stage in the discussion it would be unwise to entertain a long debate on whether tongues-speaking should have ceased with the end of the apostolic age. While there is nothing in Scripture which conclusively proves that any of these gifts are now obsolete, our concern is not for the vindication of one spiritual gift but with understanding the source and goal of all spiritual gifts.

Question 4. Help members of your group to see the big picture of this section rather than grinding to a halt trying to define "a word of knowledge," "prophecy" or "the interpretation of tongues." Paul's concern was that the Corinthians should *not* see themselves as a body of individual Christians performing their own ministries, but as members of the body *of Christ.*

Question 5. F. F. Bruce's comments on this are helpful. "No member is less a part of the body than any other member: all are necessary. Variety of organs, limbs and functions is of the essence of bodily life. No organ can establish a monopoly in the body by taking over the functions of the others. A body consisting of a single organ would be a monstrosity" *(Corinthians,* p. 121).

At this early stage in the discussion someone may confess that even though he or she is a Christian there is no evidence of a spiritual gift. This passage assures us that gifts are not something added to the believer *after* salvation as a fruit of maturity but the inheritance of every believer. An important clue to resolving this common dilemma of "I don't know what my gift is" comes from verse 1. Possibly "spiritual gifts" (12:1) should be translated "spiritual persons," since *pneumatikon* suggests "persons endowed with spiritual gifts" (F. F. Bruce, *Corinthians,* p. 116). Many people can be helped by knowing that in the totality of their persons *they* are gifts to the body.

Questions 7-8. These questions touch the nerve of the passage, Paul's repeated call to interdependence in Christ which he has been developing (chapter 8, in the exercise of freedom; chapter 9, in Paul's personal renunciation of the rights of an apostle; chapter 10, in dealing with differing consciences; and in chapter 11, in male-female relationships in the church and mutual consideration at the Lord's Supper). What makes for disunity is not diversity of expression but an arrogant, independent attitude often expressed in terms of the presumed superiority of one's own ministry. It is seldom said out loud, of course, but often thought. This passage underlines that no one has a gift alone!

Hardly anyone enjoys thinking of himself as a "weaker" (v. 22) or "unpresentable" part of the body, although some who have poor self-images in the Christian community feel this at an emotional level. Paul seems to be using *weaker* here in two senses: According to 1 Corinthians 1:26-31, some are weak according to human standards, lacking in wisdom, eloquence and social graces. In 1 Corinthians 8:7 and 9:22 Paul uses *weak* in the sense of morally or spiritually immature. Surprisingly, Paul says that such persons are indispensible to the health of the body—not just because they demand more care, but because they *are* indispensible.

"Uncomely parts" (KJV) or "unpresentable" parts may refer to the sex organs or the organs of secretion which, though hidden, are vital. God has so designed the body that we give the greatest care to the most hidden and the weakest, thereby communicating "equal concern for each other" (v. 25). It is the inspired logic of bodily life, even if it reverses the laws of human society.

Question 9. Some may propose that Paul is enumerating the *historical* sequence of gifting to the church. If this were the case, Ephesians 4:11 proposes that the apostles founded the church, and now pastor-teachers build the church. But in 1 Corinthians 12:28 that would leave the church today exclusively focused on miracle-workers, a possibility Paul would reject as unhelpful and divisive.

Most probably Paul is enumerating gifts in terms of importance. The apostles are eyewitnesses of Christ and founders of churches; prophets declare God's word with immediate relevance to life situations; teachers instruct fellow believers in Christian faith and practice; workers of miracles demonstrate God's power; healers are regularly used to bring divine healing to the sick; helpers attend to practical care as a spiritual ministry; administrators have the helmsman-leadership gift for the church; those who speak in tongues are those who are gifted to speak messages in languages not normal to the speaker, which when interpreted will edify the body (14:13).

Question 10. The New Testament does not give us a methodology for getting spiritual gifts, because it is God who orders the body and decides how each member should function. Motivation is important (how I want to serve God), but more important than desiring to express one's own gift (or potential gift) must be the desire for the health of the body.

Encouraging scriptural longings for the group or church will go a long way toward alleviating gift-frustration and preoccupation with the worth of one's own contribution. Once again, gifts emerge in mutual life and ministry and are fractions of Christ's continuing ministry in a body-life context. No one can therefore properly speak of "my" gift!

Question 11. Many groups plan a special evening once a season or year for affirming every member's contribution. Each person is bombarded by the group with statements which complete the sentence: "I find God uses you in this group through . . ." This avoids categorizing people according to gifts. An illustration or two from your present group, especially about a person whom you know feels inferior or not needed, may edify everyone and model an ongoing process.

Study 11. Love of Christ: The Most Excellent Way. 1 Corinthians 13:1-13.

Purpose: To evoke love in the Christian community as the greatest way to express interdependence in Christ.

Question 1. Many groups have people who are currently struggling with abuse from others and deep hurts. They will not easily speak of being loved. However, with some encouragement most people can find a significant "other" in their life, often in childhood, who communicated a measure of unconditional love.

Question 2. The major difficulty in leading a study on 1 Corinthians 13 is the hazard of overfamiliarity with the words and underfamiliarity with the message. Reading the passage in a fresh translation, such as Today's English Bible, or a paraphrase like Phillips or The Living Bible, may bring fresh meaning from the chapter.

Question 3. "A Christian community can make shift somehow if the 'gifts' of chapter 12 be lacking: it will die if love is absent" (F. F. Bruce, *Corinthians,* p. 124).

It is natural for us to analyze whether we "have" love by looking at the effects it has on *us.* Steer the group discussion from pointless introspection to assessing the fruits of love in the community.

Question 4. By suggesting that the group define each quality, we are trying to break the familiarity barrier with this passage. For example, *rude* (v. 5) also means behaving disgracefully or dishonorably. The unmarried adult who insists on sexual relations because of his or her "love" would, if truly loving, respect the rights and honor of the beloved. The same word is used in 1 Corinthians 7:36 for a similar indescretion. In lesser matters, courtesy has been called "love in the trifles." Much ministry simply lacks basic courtesy.

Question 6. In presenting such an absolute description of love, Paul seems to be begging the question of where we get such love. It is widely known that the special Christian word for love, *agape,* means the kind of unconditional, self-sacrificing love shown to us by Jesus. Perhaps Paul was personifying love here, as Wisdom is personified in Proverbs 8.

Questions 7-8. It is hard to maintain balance in a discussion of love and gifts. On the one hand gifts are important right now. One day God will abolish prophecy, tongues and knowledge (v. 8). In the meantime *we* must abolish the childish thinking (v. 11) that the exceptional is the best. Gifts are great for the time being. But love is greater. Prophecy without love will do nothing to build up people or edify the body (14:3) no matter how spiritual it is.

Question 9. In studying this passage it is important to keep Paul's long-term view. He is looking at the supremacy of love not only for now but forever. Faith will become sight, hope will become realization, but love will remain eternally.

Question 10. The sources of disunity in Corinth may need to be reviewed: self-promoting leaders, exaltation of the ecstatic and sensational, envy and jealousy, grouping into cliques, and "freedom" gone wild. Each of these proves to be a disguised form of self-interest.

Love offers self-realization through self-surrender. Instead of saying "I don't need you" (12:21) because you are different, love prizes others because they *are* different. Norman Wright defined love this way: "A person is in love with another individual when meeting the emotional needs of that person becomes an emotional need of his or her own life."

Study 12. Speaking for Christ: Adult Thinking and Orderly Worship. 1 Corinthians 14:1-40.

Purpose: To explore the place of inspired speech in the Christian community.

Introduction. In this study we enter deep and troubled waters for many people in the church. The attitude towards tongues and prophecy as gifts of the Spirit has been varied and controversial in church history. The lines have usually been drawn between those of a "Pentecostal" or "charismatic" persuasion and those sometimes called "traditional" or "conservative."

Some favor the continuation or revival of certain gifts of ecstatic or extemporaneous speech in congregational meetings. Others tend to downplay the importance of both tongues and prophecy and, in some cases, interpret 1 Corinthians 13:8 to mean that we now live in an age that has moved beyond these manifestations.

Some objections to tongues and prophecy today come from:

1. a psychological fear of the nonrational or intuitive side of religion;

2. an understandable distrust of any overemphasis of certain bizarre and undisciplined practices;

3. an abhorrence of an extreme theology which claims that tongues is the necessary mark of a second blessing known as Spirit-baptism;

4. a tendency toward elitism and perfectionism in some who use these gifts;

5. a desire to avoid the divisions which can follow the introduction of so-called charismatic gifts (including healing, miracles, and words of wisdom and knowledge) into body-life.

All we can ask in this one study in one chapter of 1 Corinthians is that, as far as possible, the participants put aside their traditions and prejudices and open themselves freshly to the message Paul has for us.

There has been considerable debate surrounding how we should define tongues and prophecy. For the sake of this study we will define *both* tongues and prophecy as gifts of inspired, unplanned utterances in a meeting, the former coming to the speaker in an unknown language and the latter in a known language. It is widely acknowledged that inspired preaching has some of the same prophetic dimensions of immediacy, directness and anointing from God, even though it is the fruit of careful preparation.

Question 2. Apparently, the Corinthians had elevated the gift of tongues to a much higher status than prophecy as a mark of the Christian leader, perhaps because it seemed more spiritual and "otherworldly" than speech with understandable content.

Paul has a relatively low view of the usefulness of tongues in congregational meetings because the gift fails to build up the body. However, his remarks apply only to uninterpreted tongues. When tongues were interpreted in the meeting, people were edified.

There are only hints concerning Paul's understanding of the relationship between prophecy in a local church and other revelation that has a permanent and universal force. Paul raises one standard above all utterances in public assemblies, namely the discerning gifts of the corporate body (v. 29), which presumably rely on the abiding truth of the "word of God" (v. 36). These Old Testament scriptures, together with "the Lord's command" which came to the Corinthians through the apostles' preaching and teaching (v. 37), have come down to us today in the Bible. This controlling rule over congregational word ministry has not been superseded by Paul and should not be by us.

Question 4. Our worship is meaningless or mindless when, for example, we sing hymns without paying attention to their content, or listen to sermons without applying their messages, or take communion without reflecting on its meaning.

Question 5. God used the foreign language of the invading Assyrians as a sign to unbelieving Israel that God's judgment was coming on them (Is 28:11-12). Paul concludes from this that tongues are a sign to unbelievers. Prophecy, on the other hand, is directed toward those who believe and are open to obeying God's Word.

There is an apparent contradiction between Paul's statement about the purpose of tongues and prophecy (v. 22) and his illustration about the effect of these gifts on an unbelieving visitor (vv. 23-25). This conundrum prompted the famous Bible translator, J. B. Phillips, to give up with these words: "This is the sole instance of the translator's departing from the accepted text. He felt bound to conclude, from the sense of the next three verses, that we have here either a slip of the pen on the part of Paul, or, more probably, a copyist's error" *(The New Testament in Modern English* [London: Collins, 1960], p. 552).

A better solution is to see that the apostle, oblivious to the ambiguity that would cause later interpreters so much trouble, is simply saying two different things in these verses: (1) tongues *are* for unbelievers in the sense that they are a sign of stubborn unbelief and rebellion, and (2) tongues are *not* for unbelievers in the sense that such unintelligible speech will seem strange to unbelieving visitors in the church meeting.

Question 6. The group may wish to compare the typical worship service in Corinth with the typical worship service in their church. Although the former is not necessarily normative, we should be open to learn from the model described by Paul.

Questions 7-9. There is a parallelism in verses 27-34 which is clear in Greek and in some English translations if one highlights the words *speak* (vv. 27, 29, 34) and *be* *silent* (vv. 28, 30, 34). The NIV translation has drawn out this parallelism by translating the word "speak" *(laleo)* the same way in all three verses. But it has obsured the other half of the parallelism by translating the word "be silent" *(sigao)*—which is also the same in all three verses—in three different ways: "keep quiet" (v. 28), "stop" (v. 30) and "remain silent" (v. 34). Paul is telling the Corinthians (1) when those with the gift of tongues should speak and be silent, (2) when prophets should speak and be silent and (3) when women should speak and be silent.

Question 9 could be very controversial for some in your group. However, confusion will be minimized if the group considers the following.

Your first goal should be to understand what Paul is saying in *this* passage, since it is the one being studied. You should avoid bringing in other passages prematurely.

After you feel you have a basic grasp of this passage, you can then compare Paul's teaching here with what he said in chapter 11, a passage you have studied previously. This may cause you to modify your interpretation of one passage or the other.

You should realize that one's view of women's ministries should not be based on these two passages alone. Rather, a thorough study should be made (at a later time) of all the relevant texts. However, it is humbling to realize that even those who have studied all the texts often disagree about their interpretation. If everything were clear and unambiguous, there would be no controversy!

Study 13. Hope in Christ: The Resurrection and the Life. 1 Corinthians 15:1—16:24.

Purpose: To have the hope of our resurrection become a powerful motivation in our lives.

Question 2. Although Christ's death (and burial) is obviously critical to our salvation from sin, Paul establishes the resurrection of Christ as the ultimate validation of his preaching, and of his listeners' faith and forgiveness.

The possible distaste of some Corinthians over the thought of the actual physical burial and resurrection of Christ's body would have arisen from a general abhorrence of the physical and an elevation of the spiritual dimension of reality, including the notion of the "spiritual resurrection" of Christ.

Paul lists himself as the final eyewitness of the risen Christ (though abnormally so, as his encounter was the only post-ascension appearance of Christ), presumably referring to the Damascus road experience. We have no independent details of the appearances to five hundred brethren or to James, the Lord's brother.

Question 3. Paul lists the following consequences: (1) "not even Christ has been raised" (v. 13), (2) "our preaching is useless" (v. 14), "so is your faith" (v. 14), we are "false witnesses" (v. 15), "your faith is futile" (v. 17), "you are still in your sins" (v. 17), "those also who have fallen asleep in Christ are lost" (v. 18), "we are to be pitied more than all men" (v. 19).

Question 4. "Fallen asleep" (vv. 18, 20) is obviously a metaphor for death. It refers to the temporary nature of death rather than to the gentleness of death. Many are violently martyred for Christ even today.

"Firstfruits" (v. 20) refers to the first sheaf of the harvest which was given to the Lord—a token of the larger harvest that would follow.

Question 5. It should be said that the second *all* of verse 22 is not universalistic; the next verse clearly restricts the ones "made alive" to "those who belong to him."

Question 6. For those who believe in annihilation upon death, the philosophy of verse 32 is logically and psychologically consistent, as suggested by the Preacher in Ecclesiastes 2:24.

However, the rejection of the resurrection by the Corinthians was probably more subtle, arising from the feeling that they had already experienced spiritual resurrection. Therefore, anything physical—including the physical body and physical sin—was irrelevant (see 6:12; 10:23). Hence, the moral exhortation of 15:33-34 became necessary.

In contrast to the Corinthian attitude stands Paul's willingness to be endangered every hour (v. 30), even before wild beasts in Ephesus (a figurative reference to an encounter with an angry mob, such as that described in Acts 19:23-41). Such a lifestyle only makes sense in light of the resurrection.

Much ink has been spilled in an attempt to explain Paul's seeming endorsement of the questionable practice of baptism-by-proxy. Point out to the group that the intent, nature and beneficiaries of the practice are simply unknown today, so that the force of this additional argument for the resurrection has been lost to us. Don't let the group dwell on this, or you won't have time for the clearer and more important aspects of this passage!

Question 8. Paul compares the resurrection to plant life (vv. 36-38), fleshly beings (v. 39), and heavenly and earthly bodies (vv. 40-41). The group should not only identify each of these but also explain how they support Paul's argument for the resurrection.

Spiritual body (v. 44) does not mean nonmaterial but rather a body arising from heaven rather than from the dust of the earth (v. 47).

Question 9. Paul delights in describing how the very weaknesses which the Corinthians rightly accuse him of demonstrating (1 Cor 4:9-13; 2 Cor 10:1-11) will be reversed in heaven. This will be his ultimate victory over the seductive but false Corinthian position.

Question 10. See 1 Thessalonians 4:13-18 for a parallel description of the Lord's coming.

Question 11. Paul incarnates the idea of "laboring in the Lord" in the final chapter, specifically in the context of: (1) collecting funds to aid the hungry saints of poverty- and famine-stricken Judea, (2) welcoming and assisting itinerant Christian workers, (3) remaining for a period of quality ministry in a region, (4) submitting to leaders and laborers in the work, and (5) sending gifts, both funds and friendship, to workers in isolated situations. Finally, the sympathetic reference to Apollos may represent the most powerful model of all, for it points to a spirit of unity and cooperation so lacking in the church at Corinth (see 1:12; 3:4).

Daniel G. Williams, husband and father of two, is a staff person specializing in small groups at University Chapel, Vancouver, B.C., and administrator of The Equippers, a lay training network. R. Paul Stevens, husband and father of three, is Associate Professor of Applied Theology at Regent College and Carey Hall, Vancouver, B.C., and coordinator of The Equippers.